MW00817699

BON SECOURS

ST. MARY'S HOSPITAL

GOOD HELP FOR A LIFETIME

OUR LADY OF GRACE
DONATED BY THE AUXILIARY
IN GRATITUDE TO THE
SISTERS OF BON SECOURS
OF ST. MARY'S HOSPITAL
1977

BON SECOURS

St. Mary's Hospital

GOOD HELP FOR A LIFETIME

By Mary Miley Theobald

Published by Dementi Milestone Publishing

Richmond, Virginia

First Printing

Copyright © 2016 by Bon Secours St. Mary's Hospital

All rights reserved. No part of this book may be reproduced or transmitted in any form or by any means, electronic or mechanical, including photo copying recording, or by an information storage and retrieval system, without the written permission of the Publisher.

Attempts have been made to identify the owners of any copyrighted materials appearing in this book. The editor and publisher extend their apologies for any errors or omission and encourage any copyright owners inadvertently missed to contact them.

For information write:
Dementi Milestone Publishing
1530 Oak Grove Drive
Manakin Sabot, Virginia 23103

Wayne Dementi, Project Director
Mary Miley Theobald, Author
Carol Roper Hoffler, Literati, Designer
Anne Napps, Research and editorial support

The Library of Congress Control Number: 2015954235

ISBN: 978-0-9969157-0-0

Printed in the USA

Cover photo: Allison and Brent Spiller, together with their children, Mary Michael (age 6) and Alice Holloway (age 2), meet with Dr. Sofia Teferi, Pediatric Hospitalist, in front of the St. Mary's Hospital fountain on May 12, 2015 during Allison's pregnancy with her third child. Delightfully, Edwin Gibbens Spiller was born at St. Mary's about six weeks after this photograph was taken.

This statue of Our Lady was hand carved in Italy and put in place at the hospital's opening day in 1966.

Rooted in the Past...

To the Sisters of Bon Secours and all those

who helped form the foundation of our ministry

Standing in the Present...

To all who share their gifts and

talents to provide good help today

Leading into the Future...

To those who will ensure our legacy of caring

and a future filled with hope.

 s you stand on the grounds of Bon Secours St. Mary's Hospital today, you can see the exceptional staff, facilities, technology, and structures that have led to numerous national and local accolades. The first community hospital in Richmond to achieve Magnet® recognition, a best place to have a baby, a top cardiovascular hospital and a comprehensive cancer center, St. Mary's boasts a long list of achievements. Yet, the real success of this pre-eminent medical center lies in 50 years of compassionate care, a commitment to the community and a staff dedicated to the Bon Secours mission to be *good help to those in need*.

For five decades, St. Mary's has been a place of healing and wholeness, where bells chime for each birth, where health is restored and where patients leave this world with dignity. We reflect on the courage and tenacity of the Sisters of Bon Secours and community members who helped build St. Mary's as the first fully integrated hospital, the first Catholic hospital, and the first hospital led by women in Richmond. We continue to be inspired by St. Mary's dedication to meeting people where they are and responding to their needs—first in homes and then in the 169-bed facility that has now more than doubled in size.

This book celebrates and highlights St. Mary's rich history in Richmond. But, we also want to recognize its leadership and resources, which have strengthened Bon Secours Health System as a whole.

As you may know, Bon Secours Health System did not exist when St. Mary's opened in 1966. At that time, the Sisters of Bon Secours began and led this and other hospitals, but they did not become a unified system until 1983. From that point forward, St. Mary's and its staff have provided a collaborative spirit that has helped advance the Bon Secours mission and our values, especially in the areas of technology, innovation and talent development.

Due to the success of St. Mary's, we have been able to invest in growth throughout our health system. A number of initiatives that began at St. Mary's are now integrated into our system as a whole, including the Care-a-Van mobile clinic and the focus on employee health and well-being.

St. Mary's continues to grow and innovate. Even amidst numerous changes in health care, St. Mary's and Bon Secours remain dedicated to serving those who are vulnerable, co-creating healthy communities, and putting the individual at the center of our care. We look forward to another 50 years, continuing the mission of Bon Secours and leading the way with excellence and compassion.

Richard J. Statuto
President and CEO
Bon Secours Health System

Sr. Patricia A. Eck, C.B.S.
Chairperson, Board of Directors
Bon Secours Ministries

Diocese of Richmond

Pastoral Center • 7800 Carousel Lane, Richmond, Virginia 23294-4201 • Phone: (804) 359-5661 • Fax: (804) 358-9159

Office of the Bishop

Dear Friends in Christ,

On behalf of the clergy and lay faithful of the Catholic Diocese of Richmond, we extend our heartiest congratulations to Saint Mary's Hospital on your 50th Anniversary.

In 1966 my predecessor, Bishop John J. Russell, dedicated the newly constructed Saint Mary's Hospital to serve the Central Virginia community. For 50 years Saint Mary's Hospital has been synonymous with "good help to those in need," especially the poor. The first Bon Secours Sisters to arrive in Richmond, at the request of Bishop Russell, lived near the current hospital site and provided nursing care to Richmonders in their homes. The spirit of Bon Secours, with their faith-based values, is deeply rooted in Saint Mary's Hospital and in this Central Virginia community. Saint Mary's Hospital has always been an extension of the mission of the Sisters to alleviate human suffering through the pursuit of excellence in the care of the whole person.

I commend the administrative staff, doctors, medical care providers, and the many employees of Saint Mary's Hospital who are second to none in their commitment and sincerity in the work of healing. You have gained the much deserved recognition for your services on behalf of our community.

Wishing you every success for many years to come, I remain

Sincerely yours in Our Lord,

+ Francis X. Di Lorenzo

Most Rev. Francis X. DiLorenzo
Bishop of Richmond

✦ Bon Secours ✦

More than half a century ago, three Catholic sisters from the Congregation of Bon Secours moved to Richmond to establish a hospital. For five years, they labored over every detail—formulating plans, raising money, supervising construction, purchasing equipment, hiring staff—while continuing to nurse the sick and dying in their own homes. When St. Mary's Hospital opened its doors in the early days of 1966, Richmond learned the true meaning of the French words, *bon secours*. Good help.

A hospital that reaches the age of fifty is not unusual. Some hospitals in Richmond are older than St. Mary's. Some are larger. It's not age or size or any other easily measurable feature that distinguishes St. Mary's Hospital from the rest—it is the purpose of the Sisters of Bon Secours that lies at the heart of the institution: *to provide compassionate, quality healthcare to those in need, including the poor and dying, to alleviate suffering and bring people to wholeness in the midst of pain and loss.* "It's all about bringing the love of God to people," says Sister Pat Dowling, "even in the midst of suffering when we are most vulnerable. It's our holistic approach to healing,

treating not only the body but providing spiritual, psychological, emotional, and social care. Without that, we become just another hospital focused on the bottom line."

St. Mary's was Richmond's first Catholic hospital, its first hospital run by women, and its first racially integrated hospital. In 2016, it marks the fiftieth anniversary of its founding by looking back with pride on five decades of service to the community and looking ahead to a promising future. St. Mary's Hospital has a unique story, one that began a long time ago, in a land far away.

Bon Secours is usually translated as "Good Help," but the French words carry stronger meaning than the English. *Secours*, like the English word succor, derives from the Latin verb succurrere: to run to the aid of someone. *Secours* goes deeper than mere help; it carries the sense of support, relief, and comfort for those in danger or dying.

WHAT'S THE DIFFERENCE BETWEEN NUNS AND SISTERS?

The words "nun" and "sister" are often used interchangeably, but within the Roman Catholic Church, there is an important distinction between the two. A nun lives a cloistered life; her ministry is one of prayer and contemplation. A sister lives, prays, and ministers within the world. Both are addressed as "sister." The women of Bon Secours are, properly speaking, sisters, not nuns, although many people, including the sisters themselves, refer to them as nuns in casual conversation.

Facing page: Josephine Potel, founder of Bon Secours

✦ A New Religious Order ✦

Numb after decades of bloody upheaval, all of France was struggling in 1821 to adjust to an uneasy peace. Ten years of revolutionary madness followed by fifteen years of Napoleonic warfare had brought Europe's most powerful nation to its knees. The Catholic Church, which during the Reign of Terror had seen its lands seized, its properties looted, its convents destroyed, and its clergy guillotined, had been partially restored in 1801; nonetheless, most people in France had abandoned their faith and regarded the church with suspicion. At this unlikely moment in time, a small group of young women in Paris heard God's call to start a new religious order that would serve the sick and dying.

When twenty-two-year-old Josephine Potel arrived in Paris from her rural town of Becordel in the north of France, she was shocked by the suffering and poverty she saw. Diseases spread quickly through the city, encouraged by contaminated water and congested living conditions. Epidemics were a constant

Bon Secours sisters all over the world can be recognized by this necklace. And the sisters often use the letters C.B.S.—Congregation of Bon Secours—after their names.

menace. Those who fell ill or were injured did their best to avoid the city's so-called hospitals, which were filthy, crowded deathtraps for the hopeless.

Little is known of Josephine Potel's life. Certainly she possessed a strong faith in God and a desire to serve the needy. In the course of her short time in Paris, she met several women with similar beliefs. They gathered in a small apartment on the Rue de Cassette to talk of their common desire to care for the sick and poor. They were all very young—in their late teens and twenties—but it was soon evident that Josephine was the most capable among them. She became their unofficial leader.

The women approached Father Desjardins, Vicar General of Paris, asking him to present a petition to the archbishop that would establish their group as a religious community devoted to serving the sick and dying, rich and poor alike.

Father Desjardins gave the young women a frosty reception. He'd been down this path before: an earlier attempt by some women to start a similar community had failed. But Josephine Potel was not easily discouraged, and, in the end, the vicar agreed to present their petition to the archbishop.

Hyacinth-Louis de Quelen, Archbishop of Paris, was not impressed either. Perhaps he was horrified by their request. Religious women in those days lived in convents, segregated entirely from society or, at most, venturing out briefly during daylight hours. The idea of young religious women spending their nights unsupervised in the homes of sick people, beyond the safety of convent walls, must have disturbed him. Perhaps he was suspicious of their motives. Their willingness to tend to all patients, nobles and peasants alike, did not conform to the norms of the day.

Somehow, Josephine Potel persuaded the archbishop that her vision of service came from God,

The icon on the left portrays Our Lady of Bon Secours, the Virgin Mary, holding baby Jesus. On the right is an image of Sister Angelique Geay, named superior general of the Sisters of Bon Secours in 1826 after founder Josephine Potel died. She remained in that position for thirty-four years and is honored as the principle organizer of the congregation.

First Catholic hospital in Western Hemisphere
established in Mexico City

Congregation of Bon Secours
approved

| 1099 | 1524 | 1821 | 1824 |

Crusaders created chivalric orders to care for the sick;
the earliest was the Order of St. John in Jerusalem

Bon Secours organized;
Napoleon dies

Five sisters of Bon Secours in Paris prepare to take cars, bicycles, or motorbikes to reach the sick and dying in their homes. The photo probably dates from the 1930s or 1940s.

and he granted the women a one-year probationary period to prove themselves and their faith. So in 1821, twelve young women set out to bring care and compassion to the sick, injured, and dying in their own homes, without asking whether they were Catholic, Protestant, or atheist, rich or poor.

From the start, the twelve sought to heal the whole person—body, mind, and spirit—and to bring compassion and care to everyone else in the home as well. Word spread quickly. The women remained with their patients throughout their illness, often with no place to sleep other than a pallet on the floor and nothing to eat beyond whatever food the family had. With no formal training in nursing available, they learned from one another and from experience. At the heart of their nursing was their faith: recognizing Christ in each person they tended and

affirming God's love to all. Humility, poverty, and charity were their bywords.

The archbishop could not help but be moved by their passion to serve, and he could not deny the need for their service. He accepted the twelve into the church as postulants, drew up the rules for their mission, named the new order the Congregation of Bon Secours, and appointed Josephine Potel their Superior General. The archbishop would look back on the foundation of Bon Secours as "one of the most outstanding glories" of his episcopacy.

On January 24, 1824, the twelve women—who could not resist noting the numerical coincidence with the twelve apostles—gathered at St. Sulpice where they pronounced their vows and became brides of Christ. The oldest was twenty-nine. According to custom, each received a new name.

Josephine Potel would henceforth be known as Mother Mary Joseph. Originally their habits were gray with a white fluted cap; later they adopted black robes, a veil, and white cuffs, keeping the cap.

The sisters quickly outgrew their first makeshift convent—a tiny space on the Rue de Cassette. More postulants joined. At first, mattresses on the floor accommodated them, but the numbers continued to grow. By the end of the first year, there were thirty postulants, novices, and professed sisters, and a larger house was found.

The work was hard and the hours long. Typically, the women labored every waking moment, caring for the sick, injured, and dying, with no days off. Their enemies—dysentery, typhus, smallpox, tuberculosis, pneumonia, and cholera—thrived in the filthy, crowded streets of old Paris. Naturally, the sisters were not immune. Many caught the diseases they were treating and died. On May 6, 1826, Mother Mary Joseph—Josephine Potel—succumbed to tuberculosis. She was twenty-seven years old.

The following year, the French government officially recognized the Congregation of Bon Secours. The secular government appreciated the sisters' ecumenical approach, and their humanitarian service to both rich and poor made them a valuable asset to the entire country. Inevitably, they were asked to open outposts in other cities. The usual method was to send three or four sisters to get a new community started, and then to rely on Paris to supply more as needed. They began a ministry in Lille in 1829 and in Boulogne the year after. After the potato famine struck Ireland, they established a community there in 1861. In 1870, they were invited to London. And in 1881 they came to the United States…in a providential way.

⸎

A young couple from Baltimore's Whedbe family was visiting Paris in the 1870s while on their honeymoon when the bride fell seriously ill. The sisters of Bon Secours nursed her back to health. Upon the couple's return to Baltimore, they told several local physicians about the exceptional quality of care the wife had

In 1983, the Sisters of Bon Secours proudly unveiled their new symbol, which was used to unify all the Bon Secours health care facilities in the United States. The fleur-de-lis had a strong association with the French congregation that began in Paris in 1824.

received. The doctors approached Archbishop James Gibbons, urging him to request that these sisters establish one of their communities in Baltimore.

In 1880, Archbishop Gibbons stopped in Paris on his way to Rome, where he was to be made a cardinal by Pope Leo XIII. After meeting with the sisters of Bon Secours and learning about their mission, he invited them to establish a foundation in America. They accepted. Three sisters—chosen because they spoke English—were sent to start the first American community. Mrs. John Small, a widow who had been cared for by the sisters in Ireland some years earlier, offered her own house in Baltimore as their temporary convent.

There were probably no trained nurses in Baltimore when those first three sisters arrived. Bon Secours sisters were not trained either, not in the modern sense. They had practical, on-the-job training gained by accompanying more experienced women and by listening to advice from attending physicians. Theirs was the first society of visiting nurses in the United States. Demand was so great, they could not hope to meet it.

In Baltimore, Catholics, Protestants, and Jews banded together to hold a fund-raising bazaar to help pay for a convent and headquarters, and the

Sister Rose in 1958, before the Bon Secours habit changed

in Washington DC, moving in during an epidemic of typhoid fever. In 1909, they established a convent in Detroit and ten years later, opened a home for crippled children in Philadelphia. In 1946, they started another convent in Lawrence, MA, outside Boston. Financial support for these came from the local Catholic dioceses and private donors, and sometimes from local government.

During the early twentieth century, medical practices were undergoing dramatic changes, with hospitals gradually becoming the preferred place to receive healthcare. The sisters adapted by shifting from home nursing to institutional nursing and by building their own hospitals, the first in Baltimore in 1919. What did *not* change was their holistic point of view. It was not merely the body they were treating, but the mind and spirit as well. They stayed with the terminally ill as they died, much like today's hospice caregivers. To increase their professional credentials, they established a nursing school in 1921. Their numbers grew, and in 1958, the Congregation of Bon Secours in the United States became a separate province. Baltimore had been the location of the provincial house and novitiate for Bon Secours in the United States, but in 1968, a new building in nearby Marriottsville became its physical headquarters.

Expanding their care for people in need, the sisters opened facilities wherever they could serve the poorest and most forgotten of God's people. During the twentieth century the sisters built an integrated health system that today includes twenty hospitals, eight long-term care facilities, eight assisted-living facilities, ten home health and hospice agencies, two nursing schools, numerous community health clinics, several nursing homes for the elderly, alcohol and drug abuse rehabilitation centers, and medical office complexes in Maryland, Virginia, Florida, New York, New Jersey, Pennsylvania, South Carolina, Kentucky, and Michigan.

Bon Secours: Providing good help for those in need.

sisters plunged into serving the population as they always had, without regard for religious belief or ability to pay. They also dispensed food, medicine, and clothing, and occasionally paid rent and fuel bills for the very poor. To fund their mission, they begged in market stalls for food and at drug stores for medicine. Grateful families donated what they could. Occasional bequests helped pay expenses.

Bon Secours continued to expand in America. In the summer of 1905, the sisters opened a convent

Bishop John J. Russell was overjoyed to announce in the spring of 1961 that the sisters of Bon Secours had agreed to come to Richmond to establish a Catholic hospital. He was not the first Richmond bishop to have the idea—back in the Roaring Twenties, Bishop Andrew Brennan had purchased a site. "No one doubts the need of a Catholic hospital in Richmond," he had said. "There is perhaps no city of this size in the whole country without a Catholic hospital." Unfortunately the land proved unsuitable for a hospital and had to be sold. (The site later became the location for the Mary Munford School.) Brennan's successor, Bishop Peter Ireton, tried to purchase property on several occasions, without success. Finally, after World War II had ended, he located an ideal site in Henrico County, one with high elevation that wasn't too far from the city's center.

Purchasing the land would not be simple: it consisted of thirty-two separate parcels! Patience, one of the seven heavenly virtues, played a crucial role, because it took thirteen years for the diocese to acquire all the pieces, one by one, buying a few through third parties because of old prejudices against the Catholic Church.

Finally, Bishop Ireton had the land, a sixteen-acre site at Monument and Libbie Avenues. Now he needed the money to build the hospital. He had the promise of significant financial help from Mrs. Florence H. Lawler, a widow whose family fortune came from the insurance industry. Mrs. Lawler had agreed to contribute the enormous sum of four million dollars—more than half the amount needed and equal to about 33 million dollars today. Generous donations from local Catholic parishioners and a government grant provided the remainder.

Sadly, Bishop Ireton died in 1958 before his hospital dream could be realized. He was succeeded

Bishop John J. Russell

Florence H. Lawler

The first three nuns came to Richmond to "prepare a way" for the hospital: Mother Germanus, center, Sister Mary Margaret, left, and Sister Mary of the Incarnation.

While the hospital was in the planning stages, Sister Mary Margaret, pictured here, and Sister Mary spent much of their time working with the Instructive Visiting Nurse Association, paying house calls.

by Bishop John J. Russell, who, like Ireton, hailed from Baltimore. Both men had more than a passing familiarity with the accomplishments of Baltimore's Bon Secours sisters. Russell remembered that when he was a child, the sisters had nursed his grandmother in her home, and they had cared for his sister when she contracted typhoid fever. Florence Lawler knew their healing ministry as well: the religious women had taken care of her husband in his final illness. The elderly woman happily anticipated spending her remaining years in a small apartment at the hospital built with her money, in the care of the compassionate sisters.

Bishop Russell's announcement made it official: a Catholic hospital was coming to Richmond!

On June 24, 1961, a three-sister vanguard left Baltimore and traveled to Richmond—Mother Germanus, Sister Mary Margaret, and Sister Mary of the Incarnation. The arrival date happened to coincide with the feast day of St. John the Baptist, and Mother Germanus Streett, the leader of the venture, said, "In a sense, like St. John, we came to prepare a way." All three women were experienced in hospital administration and nursing, and they knew it would take years to accomplish their assignment. Unfazed, they began by introducing themselves to a community that, aside from the 10 percent of the population that was Catholic, had never seen a religious woman in a habit. They started by ministering to the sick in their own homes, just like Josephine Potel had done in Paris all those years ago.

"Our first month in the Capitol of the State of Virginia has been completed with many firsts," wrote Mother Germanus shortly after their arrival, "and some important highlights—our first Mass, first patient, first IVNA visits [Instructive Visiting Nurse Association]. We have learned something of Southern hospitality, Southern formality, of the FFVs [First Families of Virginia], and along with it have had some good laughs."

Bishop Russell announces Catholic hospital in Richmond to be built; 3 sisters arrive

1961

1961

1961

John F. Kennedy, the first Catholic president, is inaugurated

Federal minimum wage set at $1.25/hour

Bon Secours' First Richmond Home 1961-91

The Bon Secours sisters originally lived in this small house on Bremo Road, located where the parking deck now stands.

On the afternoon of their first mass, the director of the IVNA had called on the sisters to ask if they were interested in working with his organization for the summer, because they were short-staffed. Sister Mary and Sister Mary Margaret joined at once and "were soon carrying the black bag of the public health nurse," reported Mother Germanus, "and we hope a little of Christ's love into the homes of the people of Richmond. What an opportunity to become acquainted with the Community, white and black, rich and poor alike, babies, mothers, old and young!"

The other nurses in the agency were nervous about working with sisters. "Most of them had heard only old wives tales about nuns," wrote Mother Germanus, with her usual wry humor. "One wondered if she would now have to wear long sleeves with the sisters in the office, another thought they would have to keep silence because the sisters never talk in church, etc. It must have been quite a let-down to find us quite normal." Catholics and non-Catholics alike persisted in calling the sisters "ma'am" instead of "sister," but the patients soon accepted their compassionate care.

"Richmond was the Baptist belt," says Sister Rita Thomas, remembering the early years when they wore black habits. "When the first sisters started their home nursing, people would shut the door in their faces." But as word about the gentle sisters spread through the community, suspicions faded.

Mother Germanus made a new friend when she responded to an invitation from Dr. William T. Sanger of the Medical College of Virginia to visit. She reported that they were "impressed by the cleanliness, organization, and spirit of the state institution, and how everyone spoke affectionately to this 78-year-old former president of the College… It seems that at one time he wanted Sisters to staff the Hospital because he knew they would give good care to patients. It is good to have Dr. Sanger a friend of our future hospital."

The sisters lived in a small house at 5900 Bremo Road, across from the site of the future hospital where the parking deck stands today. This would be their convent until the hospital was built and they could move inside the building itself.

Mother Germanus Streett (1899–1991)

Mary Cassandra Streett was born on May 6, 1899, to John and Ady Streett in the Maryland town named for this family of turkey farmers. A slender woman with a gentle smile and an iron will, she entered the Sisters of Bon Secours on November 21, 1923, from Baltimore, MD, and graduated from the Baltimore Bon Secours Hospital School of Nursing in 1928. Sr. Germanus worked in Baltimore and Washington, DC, before traveling to make her final profession of vows in 1932 in Paris at the Congregation Motherhouse, as was the custom in those years. In 1939 Sr. Germanus graduated from Catholic University with a BSN and later earned her Certified Nursing Home Administrator credential there. She was hospital administrator in Philadelphia, PA; Methuen, MA; and Wildwood, NJ, before coming to Richmond, VA.

Mother Germanus was among the three Sisters of Bon Secours to pioneer the congregation's foundation in Richmond. She arrived in 1961 on the feast day of St. John the Baptist. "In a sense, like St. John, I came to prepare a way," she told a reporter with a smile. From 1961-1967, she served the Richmond Bon Secours community as Superior, overseeing the logistics and funding for the construction of St. Mary's Hospital. When the hospital opened, she provided continuity as its first administrator, then returned to ministry in Philadelphia until 1982, at which time she retired to the motherhouse in Marriottsville, MD. There she continued her ministry of prayer, her beautiful needlework, and making her famous homemade fudge and tomato juice. Always keen to give credit to others, she said of St. Mary's, "Key people are what is essential to the successful operation of any hospital. And we have many such people here."

SISTER CLARE OF ASSISI MCGEE

Clare Agnes McGee was born in Philadelphia, PA, to Hugh and Anna McAuley McGee. She entered the Congregation of Bon Secours in 1952 as a registered nurse, having earned her degree at St. Mary's Hospital School of Nursing in Philadelphia. Sr. Clare was recommended to vowed religious life because of her deep faith and devotion to Catholic principles. Sr. Clare of Assisi ministered as a nurse in Darby, PA, and Rosemont, PA. In 1962, she went to Richmond to help lay the foundation for the community of the Sisters of Bon Secours and to assist with the construction of St. Mary's Hospital. Sr. Clare of Assisi was among the original eight Sisters of Bon Secours on staff in 1966 who opened St. Mary's. At her request, she was released from her vows to religious life in 1968.

SISTER MARY EMMA CARROLL (1918–2001)

Sister Mary Emma was born Mary Dorothy on December 9 to Lewis Joseph and Mary Ann Daggett in Branchdale, PA, in the year of the infamous flu pandemic. She entered the Congregation of Bon Secours in 1935 and professed her perpetual vows in 1943. Sr. Mary Emma graduated as an RN from the Baltimore Bon Secours Hospital School of Nursing in 1942 and soon after entered upon a second career as an X-ray technician. She served in Grosse Pointe, MI, then was a member of the first group of sisters assigned in 1965 to staff the new St. Mary's Hospital in Richmond. Sr. Mary Emma ministered at St. Mary's Hospital until 1971. After Richmond, she served in Marriottsville, MD; Darby, PA; and Rosemont, PA, before returning to Grosse Pointe. "I will always remain faithful to our Holy Father and the Church in Rome…I love Bon Secours dearly," she once said. Sr. Mary Emma was an avid sports fan and a life-long supporter of the Philadelphia Phillies. She went to her eternal reward November 3, 2001.

✦ The New Hospital ✦

In the 1950s, institutional healthcare in Richmond consisted of the Medical College of Virginia, established before the Civil War, and a number of smaller hospitals that were "owned by surgeons with big egos and strong personalities," says Dr. Tommy Davis, whose list included St. Luke's, Stuart Circle, St. Elizabeth's, Grace, and Johnston-Willis. The private hospitals were "closed staff," meaning they excluded competing doctors. "The only open staff was Retreat, which was an old hospital, and Richmond Memorial," he said. "The others were run with an iron hand by the surgeons. After World War II, the population of Richmond increased, and there was a need for more open staff facilities." Typically, doctors saw patients in their offices, and whenever a patient required hospitalization, the doctors used whichever hospital they were affiliated with. The concept of physicians' offices attached to hospitals did not yet exist, so doctors spent a good deal of time driving back and forth to see patients, day or night, as needed.

Doctors new to Richmond found opportunities to practice very restricted. "To practice medicine in Richmond in the 1950s and 1960s, you had to be at MCV or know surgeons or families who owned the [private] hospitals," says Dr. George Knaysi.

St. Mary's would become Richmond's third and largest "open hospital," accepting all qualified physicians who applied for affiliation. "This was very groundbreaking," says Dr. Don Seitz. "They were so welcoming to physicians of all races and religions. The sisters made no distinction between races, and Jewish doctors felt very welcome. That just wasn't true of other hospitals."

"Many doctors couldn't use the private hospitals," recalls Dr. Larry Zacharias. "I started practicing in 1962 with my older brother, who began in the fifties, mainly at Richmond Memorial and Retreat. We were looking forward to St. Mary's because we're Catholic, and we knew the nuns would do an excellent job. When St. Mary's opened, it opened up the practice of medicine in Richmond. Other hospitals had to improve to keep up with the brand new facilities. Other hospitals didn't have all the specialties covered."

The new hospital would be built on a tract of land in what was then known as Richmond's far west end. "The city ended at the Boulevard when I was a boy," remembers Dr. Davis. "West of the Boulevard was a big farm. Monument Avenue was a two-lane road with no traffic. I used to hunt crows on the property where the hospital stands today, to practice my shooting."

Dr. Thomas D. Davis, Jr., a gastroenterologist, was one of the first doctors to affiliate with St. Mary's Hospital. Every hospital was required to have a medical library for the staff to read the latest journals, and Dr. Davis was given the job of starting up St. Mary's library. "Sister Mary Monica, a very strong-willed lady in every regard, let it be known that she had library experience, which I did not. The library was to be funded through staff donations. I thought the hospital should fund the library, and I pushed until the administrator agreed. Sister Mary Monica did *not* agree, and she told me 'Dr. Davis, we're going to do it your way and pray every day for the Lord to change your mind.'"

Facing page: Sister Frances Helen, left, and Mother Germanus demonstrate the swivel windows overlooking the future parking lot in the spring of 1965.

Bishop Russell, seated left, and Mother Germanus, beside him, signing the contracts for St. Mary's. Standing behind the bishop is Monsignor Harold Nott, left, pastor of Lynchburg's Holy Cross Church and diocesan director of hospitals, who was instrumental in Florence Lawler's interest in a Catholic hospital, and Monsignor Ernest Unterkoefler, chancellor of the Richmond diocese. Sister Mary Margaret and Sister Mary of the Incarnation, far right, look on.

"In the end, it's about the people. I've been a patient [at St. Mary's] more than once, and I realized that the people you think are the big shots aren't as important to you as the less exalted people who are with you at night when you are cold or hurting. You learn a lot when you're on the receiving end. A lot of people at St. Mary's have been here many years, and when you're sick, their kindness goes a long way."

— Dr. George Knaysi

Although Bishop Russell was the ranking Catholic in the Richmond diocese, when it came to the hospital, Mother Germanus ran the show. The original plans called for a 160-bed facility with an assembly area for two hundred, an outpatient department, a surgery department with six operating rooms, an obstetrical unit with three delivery rooms, a pediatrics department, an emergency department, a chapel open to all faiths, a pharmacy, a laundry, an autopsy room, a museum, and a nurses' training school. Newspapers of the day remarked favorably on the modern features, such as central air-conditioning and a new form of heating and cooling that replaced radiators and air ducts with a grid of pipes in the ceiling, allowing each room's temperature to be controlled individually. The hospital would be staffed by a minimum of twenty-five sisters, all of whom were registered nurses, plus an equal number of lay nurses and some practical nurses.

"Mother Germanus was very personable," recalls Monsignor Thomas Shreve, a retired priest who served as the bishop's secretary during the time St. Mary's Hospital was being planned and built. "Very friendly with everyone, very bright, very clear about what she wanted. A real businesswoman. She knew what sort of hospital should be built, and she surprised the architects [Ballou and Justice] by refusing some of the things they drew. There was a big tussle about the fountain out front. 'We can't afford it,' they said. 'No, the fountain will take care of the air-conditioning unit,' Mother Germanus insisted." She had her way.

An even bigger tussle came when Mother Germanus had her first glimpse of the architectural drawings. As was typical of hospitals and other public buildings in the South, the rest rooms, patients' rooms, and waiting rooms were segregated by race. Mother Germanus was having none of that. Legend has it she made her point in dramatic fashion by tearing up the architects' plans, and when pressure

Monsignor Thomas Shreve

was brought to bear on the church to go along with local custom, she stiffened the bishop's spine and held her ground. The sisters of Bon Secours served everyone without regard for race, religion, or ability to pay—period. St. Mary's would be the region's first integrated hospital, not only within its physical facilities, but with its doctors and nurses as well. The principled stand came at a price: some physicians and patients refused to use an integrated hospital.

In 1972, the fountain along Monument Avenue was dedicated. Mrs. Florence Lawler had requested in her will that a fountain of "handsome proportions" be built at the hospital, and Bon Secours was determined to carry out her wishes. The auxiliary donated the funds. The fountain is on a strip of land beside the hospital leased from the city of Richmond for $1/year for 99 years.

"The nuns showed something that hadn't been shown heretofore, and whether it's spunk, whether it's courage, whether it's raw fortitude, whatever it is, it's good."

— L. Douglas Wilder,
governor of Virginia
1990–1994

"When the hospital was built, there was a door at the end of the even side of 2N that led into the chapel balcony. On holy days such as Easter and Christmas, the door was opened and patients and the staff could hear the mass and beautiful music fill the halls. Also, patients and families could enjoy the mass and their privacy."

— Earlean Didlake,
unit secretary

Douglas Wilder, Virginia's first African-American governor, recalls the interest in the black community when word spread that the new hospital would be integrated. "I grew up on Church Hill and St. Philip's was the hospital designated for Negroes," he said. "I had pretty much given up on the system working at all. …But when you saw this magnificent edifice being constructed and learned it was not cordoned off for certain people, that said someone's finally got it right. St. Mary's was very, very instrumental in showing that things could work…it was an adrenaline shot that sparked a continued interest in improving [race relations]." Wilder, who was beginning his law practice at the time St. Mary's opened, would occasionally visit African-American clients in the hospital. "I inquired about their treatment, and I never heard any complaints."

Having been a hospital administrator since 1949, Mother Germanus knew her way around medical equipment. "We never took any salesman talk," she told a reporter with a twinkle in her eye. "We always asked where the equipment was being used, and we went and saw it. We got to talk with the people who used it and found out how well they liked it."

Among Mother Germanus's many talents was an eye for interior design: the "bright blues, soft green, pinks, and yellows" described in the newspaper were her idea, as was the lobby with earth tones accented with bronze, the first-floor chapel with lavender and pale green stained-glass windows and deep purple carpeting. She placed German and Italian wooden statues throughout the building and ordered brushed chrome furniture and upholstered chairs and sofas that were brown, blue, gold, black, and red.

Richmond's newest hospital had another unique feature: a convent on the seventh floor where the sisters would live. It was designed much like a dormitory, with individual bedrooms and a communal kitchen, living room, dining room, and private chapel. A large picture window overlooked the city skyline to the east.

On the second floor, architects were instructed to design a small apartment for Florence Lawler, the elderly benefactor who was planning to move

The original lobby was a product of local talent. Harvey McWilliams of Miller & Rhoads was the interior decorator who chose the leather sofas and matching chairs and benches, as well as the draperies that covered the glass wall along the front entrance. The unusual screens separating the lobby from the main corridor were designed by local sculptor Dick Cossitt. The planters are original designs made by Jim Purlizer, a potter at the Virginia Museum of Fine Arts. William Gaines is the artist who painted the picture hanging over the fireplace.

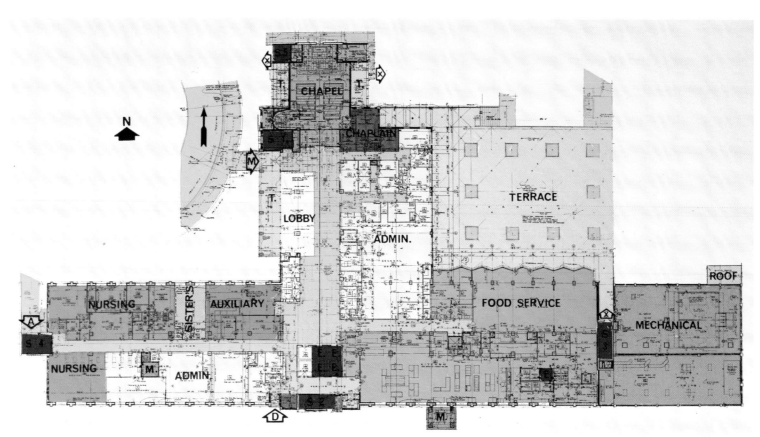

FIRST FLOOR PLAN

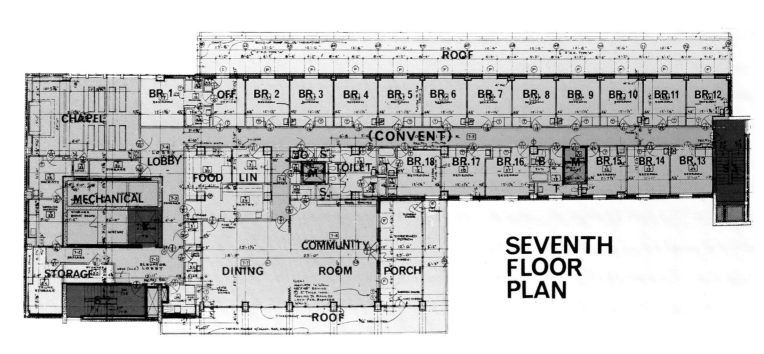

SEVENTH FLOOR PLAN

The architectural firm of Ballou and Justice drew the plans for the original portion of St. Mary's, with architects Louis Ballou and John Allen leading the process. While the firm had a strong record in designing medical facilities throughout Virginia, the convent feature was a first.

from Florida to spend her final years at the hospital. Unfortunately, Mrs. Lawler died in 1962 without ever having seen the results of her generosity. The apartment was built anyway and used for church leaders or private VIP patients.

The sisters hired Kellstrom and Lee, a company with a solid track record in building hospitals, to build St. Mary's. They broke ground on March 19, 1963. Marian Mahon, a longtime volunteer at St. Mary's, happened to attend the ceremony. "My husband was the editor of the *Catholic Virginian*," she said, "so he was there to report on the event. I came along." It was raining, so the ceremony was cut short.

Sister Elaine Davia remembers what the construction site looked like when she arrived in Richmond in 1964 as a nineteen-year-old contemplating joining a religious order. "It was a big hole in the ground with all these pipes sticking out.

Mother Germanus turns over the first shovel of earth while Bishop Russell and Father Harold Nott look on.

Bishop Russell unveils the artist's rendering of the hospital at the groundbreaking ceremony on a rainy spring day in 1963.

The construction firm of Kellstrom and Lee built the original portion of St. Mary's in 1963–66.

Valentine Richmond History Center

"One [terminally ill] patient told me he had grown up in a house that had once stood where the hospital is today. He was proud that he'd lived there and content to know that he would die in the same place he was born."

—Sister Rose Marie Jasinski

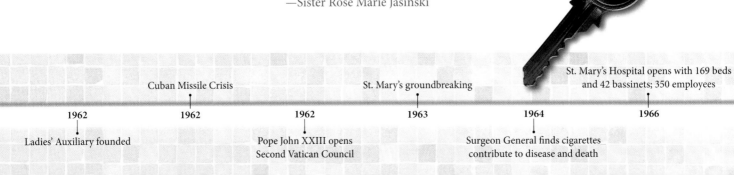

Cuban Missile Crisis

St. Mary's groundbreaking

St. Mary's Hospital opens with 169 beds and 42 bassinets; 350 employees

1962   1962   1962   1963   1964   1966

Ladies' Auxiliary founded

Pope John XXIII opens Second Vatican Council

Surgeon General finds cigarettes contribute to disease and death

Sister Frances Helen Lewandowski and Sister Clare of Assisi McGee inspect the roof.

Dr. Larry Zacharias was one of the first doctors to bring patients into St. Mary's. He served as president of the medical staff from 1984–87.

Nearly five years ago, two Bon Secours nuns and I came to Richmond to build a hospital. We had little other than our personal belongings and the promise of a warm welcome to the community.

On Sunday, January 9, St. Mary's Hospital came to full reality and, beyond a doubt, the initial warmth of our welcome had mushroomed into a whole-hearted, gracious and over-whelming reception. We cannot adequately express our appreciation of the cordiality extended by our new neighbors who attended our dedication ceremonies and toured St. Mary's. We wish to acknowledge gratefully the kindness of many friends and members of the business community who sent flowers and messages of good will.

On behalf of the staff of St. Mary's Hospital and myself, I want to convey a heartfelt thank you to the community. We will dedicate ourselves to repaying this generous welcome with the only coin of the realm we possess—service to the sick and suffering members of this community that has so graciously opened its arms to us.

Our prayers and our service will always be with our fellow Richmonders and the doors of St. Mary's always open to them.

Mother Germanus,
Administrator,
St. Mary's Hospital

They needed the extra pipes because they'd discovered how high the water table was." While the concrete was being poured, Sister Rose O'Brien placed a small statue of St. Mary and some holy water into the foundation.

Monsignor Shreve is one of very few people still living who attended the January 9, 1966 dedication of the finished building. "The papal nuncio came down from Washington," he recalls, "and Bishop Russell and Cardinal [Lawrence] Shehan were there. After the dedication, everyone went to a different wing and sprinkled holy water. I remember one of the altar boys serving the nuncio that day dropped and broke the nuncio's crozier [staff]." An army band from Fort Lee played the national anthem; a color guard from Benedictine College Preparatory School raised the flag; the St. John Vianney Seminary choir provided the music. Guided tours for the public followed.

Father J. Scott Duarte was a teenager when his father took him to the dedication. "It was exciting," he remembers. "Bishop Russell and Monsignor Sullivan sprinkled holy water in every room of the hospital, determined that every room would be blessed. The Catholic community was rather small then, and this gave us a tremendous sense of pride that we could accomplish something so important."

Dr. Zacharias also attended the dedication, and he brought his first patient into the hospital a few days later. "Compared to other hospitals, St. Mary's was all new and shiny. St. Luke's and Stuart Circle seemed really old by comparison. Having an ER in the West End was very convenient. We no longer had to go northside or downtown to MCV to see our patients. There were no ER specialists back then; doctors had to go into the hospital with their own patients."

Tours of the hospital were conducted for the community during the week following the dedication. The first floor contained the lobby, cafeteria, snack bar, and gift shop, plus business offices, a doctors' lounge, and a library.

Letter to the Richmond community, printed in the Richmond Times-Dispatch, January 19, 1966.

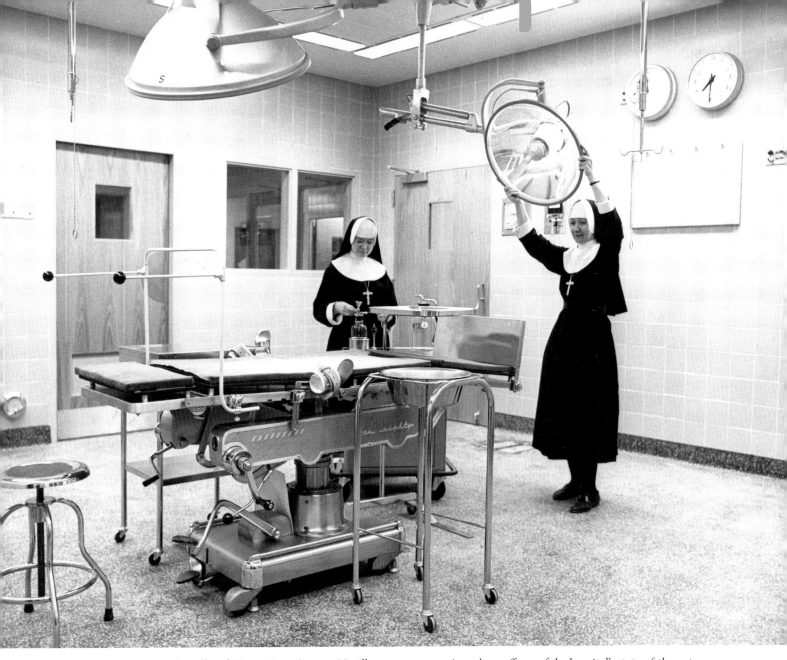

Sister Mary Emma Carroll and Sister Mary Gemma Neville, surgery supervisor, show off one of the hospital's state-of-the-art operating rooms as the hospital prepares to open.

The second floor opened with fifteen bedrooms and the heating and air-conditioning equipment, as well as a balcony entrance to the chapel. The third floor was devoted to obstetrics with four delivery rooms and six labor rooms. The fourth and fifth floors were for general nursing, with an intensive-care unit on the fourth. Pediatrics dominated the sixth floor, including a playroom and four rooms with beds for a parent to stay with the child. The convent occupied the seventh floor.

The three sisters who had been living in the temporary convent across the street from the construction site—Mother Germanus, Sister Clare of Assisi McGee, and Sister Rita Thomas (then known as Sister Xavier)—moved into their new convent on the seventh floor in December 1965. The move came with some excitement: their elevator, crammed with sisters and luggage, got stuck between floors and the sisters had to be rescued. That Christmas, they followed Virginia's eighteenth-century custom of placing candles in each of the convent's windows.

The convent floor had enough rooms for eighteen women. Mother Germanus and Sisters Clare and Rita were soon joined by five more, all experienced registered nurses: Sister Bernadette Maureen Rogers, Sister Mary Monica Curley, Sister Mary Emma Carroll, Sister Mary Gemma Neville, and Sister Rose O'Brien. Sister Rita would supervise the nurses; Sister Rose, a medical technologist, would supervise the pathology department; Sister

Charlie Carter

Charlie Carter of Maintenance remembered one of his unusual duties when the hospital first opened. "I repaired a lot of rosary beads. The sisters wore them around their waists. They weren't used to the L-shaped door handles. The rosaries were always breaking. I made more 9-bead and 11-bead sets. You see, I'm Baptist, and I didn't know each had to be in sets of 10." Carter, an electrician, spent his entire career at St. Mary's, beginning in 1965 when he helped build the original hospital. He retired in 2014.

Mary Gemma would supervise the operating rooms; Sister Mary Monica would handle medical records. "The heart and pulse of any hospital are its medical records," she liked to say, "and it's important we keep them at our fingertips. These new systems are wonderful."

Sister Mary Emma, an X-ray technician who was reassigned from Michigan, was delighted to find herself in Richmond on a mild and sunny winter day. "The weather is wonderful," she told a reporter. "It was so cold and snowing when we left Michigan. Already I love it here!"

More than sisters and nurses are necessary to run a hospital. Dr. Edwin Kendig was named chief of staff; Dr. Charles Zacharias, chief of medicine; Dr. Charles Riley, chief of surgery; Dr. David Forrest, chief of obstetrics and gynecology; Dr. Robert Hoffman, chief of pediatrics; and Dr. Robert Duley, chief of general practice. Janet Kincaid was named executive housekeeper; Luther Canada, maintenance engineer; Margaret Floyd, business manager; Abbie Acey, chief admitting officer; James Thompson, personnel director, and Benjamin Splan, purchasing agent. Monthly payroll amounted to $30,000 for a staff of 350.

Sister Rita, who was at that time the director of nursing, remembered hiring her first employees. "We had a good and close relationship with our personnel, one that has lasted through the years… Prior to the opening of the hospital, two young, timid, non-Catholic nurses came to apply for jobs. I was delighted. They were hesitant, not knowing what to expect of the sisters. One stayed on full-time for years as a head nurse. The other worked for years, also as a head nurse…St. Mary's was the first hospital in the area to be integrated. In fact…we opened with 100 percent integration."

Medicare and
Medicaid begin

Intensive care unit opens

1966

1966

1966

1966

Bon Secours has 152 sisters
in the U.S.

School of Practical
Nursing begins

For convenience, the convent's location couldn't be beat. The commute to work could literally be measured in the number of seconds it took the elevator to reach the correct floor, but Sister Rita's morning commute took a bit longer. "I used to walk down from the seventh floor every morning, stopping into each unit, until I got to the [ground-floor] office."

Opening the hospital was a gradual process that took several weeks, but on its very first day in operation, February 15, 1966, St. Mary's admitted thirteen patients.

When St. Mary's opened in 1966:

- The staff numbered 350. In 2015, there were 2,329.

- The hospital employed about 50 nurses, all female. Today there are 1,200 nurses, counting both full- and part-time, men and women.

- The going rate of pay for dietary and housekeeping staff in Richmond was 60 cents an hour. "We opened with a $1.25 minimum," one sister recalled.

New Hospital Cradles Its First Baby -- A Boy!

Little Patrick Anthony Zohab is all by himself in his pink nursery at St. Mary's Hospital.

But the rollicking 6-pound 6-ounce baby has a right to be a guest of honor — he's the first baby born in the new hospital.

Son of Mr. and Mrs. Arthur J. Zohab, Patrick was born yesterday on another famous birthday in the new maternity section of the hospital.

So far, only two departments are open on a limited basis, the medical surgical ward and maternity, which opened Monday.

But for now, only Patrick holds reign. And, according to the nurses in the maternity ward:

"He's getting lots of tender, loving care."

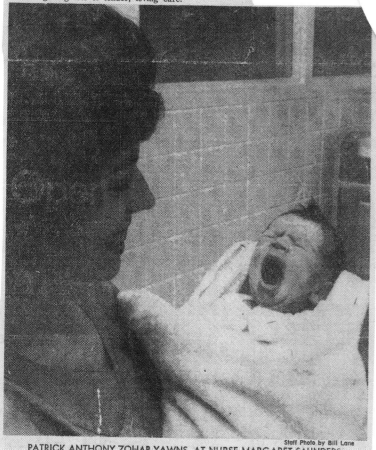

Staff Photo by Bill Lane

PATRICK ANTHONY ZOHAB YAWNS AT NURSE MARGARET SAUNDERS
The Youngster Has the St. Mary's Nursery to Himself

The first baby born at St. Mary's was Patrick Anthony Zohab on February 22, 1966. The Zohab family, members of St. Anthony's Maronite Catholic Church, still lives in Richmond. Patrick Anthony, the baby boy who had the nursery all to himself that day, works for CarMax today and lives in Gum Spring. His mother, Barbara Zohab, remembers her stay at St. Mary's very well. "All the nurses were wonderful," she said. "They treated us like royalty. St. Mary's is still where I prefer to go."

SISTER MARY GEMMA NEVILLE (1925–2007)

Mary Jo Neville grew up in a family of fifteen children born to Frederick and Ella
Sigfrid Neville. Born on January 18, 1925, Mary Jo first encountered the Sisters of
Bon Secours as a young child. Her mother was quite ill, and a Bon Secours sister was
sent to nurse Mrs. Neville and provide comfort to the Baltimore family. After high
school, Mary Jo entered the Congregation of Bon Secours and made her perpetual
profession of vows to religious life in 1951. A lifelong learner, Sr. Mary Gemma earned
her RN from the Baltimore Bon Secours Hospital School of Nursing in 1948, her
masters in divinity in 1979, her clinical pastoral education certification, and later
a doctorate of ministry. Sr. Mary Gemma served in the Philadelphia area, then in
Methuen, MA, where she was living when called upon to advise with the planning
and opening of St. Mary's Hospital in Richmond. She was among five sisters of
Bon Secours sent in 1965 to assist the three already working there. When the hospital
opened, she supervised the surgical unit until she returned to Methuen in 1969.
Sr. Mary Gemma would go on to minister in Marriottsville, MD; Chicago, IL; and
Charleston, SC. She played the guitar, wrote poetry, and had a great sense of humor.
"Our Mission as Sisters of Bon Secours is geared toward wholeness, giving not only
physical and emotional comfort to our patients, but spiritual consolation as well…
a Trinitarian Relationship between God, self, and others," she said. Sr. Mary Gemma's
sister, Angela Neville (1928–2010), was also a Sister of Bon Secours.

Sister Mary Catherine Rogers
(Sister Bernadette Maureen) (1935–2010)

According to family lore, Mary Catherine Rogers was born with complications at the Bon Secours Hospital in Baltimore on December 29, 1935. Sister Liborius Morrison (1897–1990) took the fragile infant and placed her on the chapel altar to dedicate her to God. She was the daughter of William and Katheryn Phelan Rogers and the niece of another sister of Bon Secours, Sr. Chantal Rogers (1895–1963). After high school, when Mary Catherine expressed her desire to enter the convent, her mother told her, "They placed you in the Baby Jesus manger on the altar in the chapel. They put a spell on you—that's why you want to join them!" Mary Catherine entered the Congregation of Bon Secours after graduating from the Baltimore Bon Secours Hospital School of Nursing in 1957. She took the name Sr. Bernadette Maureen after her patron saint, Bernadette, and earned her BSN from Catholic University in 1963. She made her final profession of vows in 1965. She served as a staff nurse and instructor at the Baltimore hospital before being sent in late 1965 to St. Mary's Hospital to help with its opening. Sr. Bernadette Maureen would minister at St. Mary's until 1973. Then she served at Grosse Pointe, MI, for ten years until selected to the Congregation of Bon Secours leadership team and sent to work in Rome. After her six-year term, she returned to the United States and worked in Marriottsville, MD; Charleston, SC; and Venice, FL. At some point in the 1990s, she returned to her baptismal name and was known as Sr. Mary Catherine until her full communion with God on May 5, 2010.

One of the first tasks Mother Germanus tackled upon her arrival was the creation of a women's auxiliary. Realizing how important it was to win over Richmond society, she began by inviting Catholic women from each of the eighteen parishes in the diocese to join a hospital support group. They, with a significant contingent of Jewish women, formed the nucleus of the auxiliary. Father Shreve remembers its formation. "I believe the Catholic and Jewish women, as minorities in Protestant Richmond, felt a connection. It wasn't long before Protestant women joined too." Father Duarte agrees. "St. Mary's broke down a lot of barriers between people of different faiths."

"The volunteers were our public ambassadors," remembers Sister Rita. The organizational meeting in January 1962 at the John Marshall Hotel brought out 950 women, a number that shocked even the most optimistic of supporters. The mayor's wife, Mrs. Morrill M. Crowe, agreed to become the group's first president. They decided that their initial fund-raiser would be a bazaar.

Mother Germanus probably suggested the idea—bazaars had raised money for Bon Secours facilities back in Baltimore ever since 1884. With a nod to the sisters' French origins, the auxiliary organized a Parisian Flea Market to be held in the ballroom of the Altria Theater, then known as the Mosque, on November 22, 1962. Twenty-one booths sold every sort of donated merchandise imaginable: children's clothing, dolls, needlework, books, hobbies, hats, jewelry, art, silver, handmade items, Christmas decorations, handbags, and food, with a white elephant booth to cover anything that defied categorization.

The celebrity booth garnered the most publicity with merchandise contributed from movie stars like comedian Bob Hope, singer Frank Sinatra, and actress Loretta Young, who sent a cocktail hat with white ostrich plumes that she had worn. Bon Secours sisters from all over the world sent items: a llama rug

One of the first things Mother Germanus, left, did after arriving in Richmond was to organize the ladies' auxiliary. The line to get into their first bazaar at the Mosque snaked around the block. The successful fund-raising event was held for six years.

Mrs. Morrill M. Crowe, wife of Richmond's mayor, headed the hospital's auxiliary for its first few years. Pictured here with pen in hand, she is working with Mother Germanus and others on the fund-raising bazaar. Mrs. Edmund Schmitz is at the far left; Mrs. Herman Gundlach, is standing; Mrs. George Brooks is seated far right.

Sister Frances Helen works at the Parcel Post booth at the 1964 bazaar with Mrs. John Smorto and Mrs. E. Martin Reyes.

Mayor Eleanor Sheppard, Richmond's first female mayor, cuts the ribbon to open the 1963 Parisian Flea Market. To the right of the mayor is Mrs. Peter Pastore; to the left is Mrs. Arthur Gallagher and Mother Germanus. Six hundred volunteers worked on the flea market, which made $13,000, the equivalent of more than $100,000 today.

from Peru, a camel seat from Egypt, a crimson velvet little-boy suit worn by Prince Albert of Monaco, and a crucifix from Rome. On the day of the bazaar, the line to enter the Mosque theater stretched for blocks. The ladies expected hundreds—they got thousands. The event was such a success—they cleared more than $10,000, or about $80,000 today—that they repeated the event for the next five years. Mrs. Crowe proudly told a reporter, "We made so much money, we had to have the police come to guard the 'take.'"

After the hospital opened, the auxiliary provided a wide array of services. Volunteers worked four-hour shifts staffing the reception desk, ringing up sales in the gift shop, delivering flowers, mail, and newspapers to patients, knitting pink and blue baby caps, taking pictures of newborns for the proud parents, assisting with discharged patients, helping maintain medical records, working in the medical library, delivering lab specimens and reports, and handling television rentals. Gene Oakey, a volunteer since 1972, remembers television rentals costing $2.06 a day with tax. "We'd activate the black and white TVs in the patient's room. Some time in the 1980s, we ceased to charge for that service." Mary Ann Sheehan, who began volunteering with her mother before the hospital was built, says, "I love to take flowers to patients, and I like helping people to their cars—they are so happy to go home. Especially with the new babies."

ST. MARY'S HOSPITAL · RICHMOND, VIRGINIA

This is to Certify that

_____

IS A *Founding* MEMBER
ST. MARY'S HOSPITAL AUXILIARY
FOR THE YEAR 1962

CHARTER MEMBER

BISHOP OF RICHMOND
AND SPIRITUAL DIRECTOR

The purpose of the Auxiliary is to cooperate with the Sisters of Bon Secours in any way that they may deem beneficial to St. Mary's Hospital. Members share in the prayers and good works of the Sisters wherever they labor for the sick throughout the world.

Volunteers Marcie Sabatini, left, and Nancy Plageman work at the flower shop, creating cheerful floral arrangements and delivering them to the patients' rooms.

Gift shop volunteers pose in 1999 with Sister Rose.

"Volunteering is very rewarding to me. It gives me a reminder in my life that there is somebody else in control."

—Mary Washbourne, volunteer since 1968

Initially, the volunteers wore pink pinafores over their own white blouses. In 1972, when the auxiliary expanded to include men, the men wore white jackets. Today, everyone wears Bon Secours blue uniforms.

Mary Washbourne started volunteering in 1968. Because she worked at a day job, her volunteer hours came at night in the Emergency Room. "Three of us were assigned to the ER from 5:30 to 8:00 if they weren't busy, to 10:00 or 11:00 if they were. We loaded supply carts, helped the receptionist, talked to the children with injuries, took patients upstairs, assisted the doctor—some things we wouldn't be allowed to do today. The ER was smaller in those days. There were curtains to divide the patients and there were women in labor. It was noisy. We kept the coffeepot in the waiting area going. Then in the 1980s, we moved from ER to General Services where I am today."

The money raised each year was hugely important to the hospital. It did not buy frills. In the early years, volunteers liked to keep the annual total a secret until the day they presented a large check to the administrator. In 1979, for example, auxiliary funds bought an electro-cardiology machine for the Health Wagon, a heart and respiratory monitor for pediatric patients, a microfiche camera system, surgical and anesthesia supplies, an electronic security system, and a freezer and temperature recorder for storing plasma in the blood bank.

A junior auxiliary of high school girls volunteered during the summer months. In their first decade, the girls, known as Bonnies, contributed 12,000 hours. Today the group includes boys and girls of all religions and races, aged fifteen and up. They are called Junior Volunteers, and they perform much the same functions as the adults in General Services and at the information desk.

ST. MARY'S HOSPITAL VOLUNTEER AUXILIARY PRESIDENTS

1962–1964	Mrs. Morrill M. Crowe
1964–1965	Mrs. E. Milton Farley, III
1965–1966	Mrs. William J. Doran, Jr.
1966–1968	Mrs. W. Sarsfield Nott
1968–1969	Mrs. William P. Cooksey
1969–1971	Mrs. Joseph Bandrofcheck
1971–1973	Mrs. Joseph K. Fineran
1973–1975	Mrs. John J. Zenner, Jr.
1975–1977	Mrs. Edmund G. Schmitz
1977–1979	Mrs. Harvey C. Higgerson
1979–1981	Mrs. Lawrence H. Haskin, Jr.
1981–1983	Mrs. Joseph B. Elliott
1983–1985	Mrs. Robert J. Leahy
1985–1987	Mrs. James H. Kirby
1987–1989	Mrs. Dan Miller
1989–1991	Mrs. Charles P. Cooke, Jr.
1991–1993	Mrs. Robert S. Campbell
1993–1995	Theodore Carron
1996–1997	Bonnie Pollack
1998–2000	Nancy Plageman
2001–2003	Payson Jones
2004–2005	Peggy Williams
2006–2007	Joseph Borzelleca
2008	John Chaich
2009–2010	Joe Lynch
2011–2012	Jerry Katz
2013–2014	Frank Brogdon
2015–present	Pam Spence

Dr. Joseph Borzelleca, professor emeritus at the Medical College of Virginia, tells Anne Napps about his twelve years of volunteer work at the surgical waiting area of St. Mary's. "I work two days a week, from 7:30 to 6:00, and am never tired. I feel great going home. It's one of the finest things I've ever done."

Volunteers Bettylou Gevich and Ethel Nelmes answer questions and direct visitors.

"This is my second home," says **Lloyd Bell,** who, at 95, is St. Mary's oldest volunteer. For the past 35 years, he has volunteered at the hospital where his late wife worked as a nurse. "She became a nurse after the children were grown. It was the realization of her dreams." They volunteered together, twice a week, until her death six years ago. "When I lost my wife, I stepped up my volunteering from two to four days a week. Then I began to have health issues, and had to cut back to two days. I got better, so I asked the doctor for a note to say I was healthy enough to get my days back. Now I work Mondays, Wednesdays, and Fridays. It gives me a good feeling: Whatever you do to the least of these, you do it to me."

✦ A Progressive Hospital ✦

The Congregation of Bon Secours had a custom in those days of reassigning their leaders every six years, so in the summer of 1967, after Mother Germanus had been in Richmond for six years, she was transferred to Philadelphia to continue her ministry there. An editorial in the *Richmond Times-Dispatch* praised her accomplishments: "A woman of exceptional executive gifts and quietly charming personality, with an unusual sense of humor and quick wit, Mother Germanus radiated good will and warmth wherever she went." The highly capable Sister Rita Thomas, a tiny woman with a big smile who was serving as director of nursing, took her place in both the position of religious superior and hospital administrator.

History remembers the 1960s as a time of great change and upheaval—the Cold War, race riots, assassinations, campus unrest, and antiwar demonstrations—and so it was as well for the Catholic Church. The Second Vatican Council, popularly known as Vatican II, transformed the church in ways that affected the Congregation of Bon Secours. Since its start in Paris, Bon Secours sisters had been more independent than other religious women, and when Vatican II gave nuns the option of modernizing their dress, the sisters of Bon Secours decided to make their traditional habit optional.

For some, the change was welcome. "I wasn't too crazy about it [the habit]," remembers Sister Jean Aulenbeck. "Most of us were delighted not to have to wear the headgear—I was forever jabbing myself with pins. And those rosaries were always getting caught on bedside railings." Others, like Sisters Mary Monica and Rose, declined the offer and continued to dress in the familiar white habit for the remainder of their lives. But wearing street clothes made it harder to distinguish the sisters at St. Mary's from other hospital employees.

Sister Rita Thomas opened St. Mary's hospital and served as its second administrator after Mother Germanus was reassigned.

"When you enter a convent, it's like the army or navy, you're just sent. You don't make the decisions. My life hasn't been planned; I was called to serve, and I did the best I could."

—Sister Rita

"Our [Bon Secours] sisters are more independent minded, compared to other communities. We are not as restricted. We are trusted to make our own decisions based on maturity and ability."

—Sister Vicky Segura

Facing Page: After Vatican II made the wearing of habits optional, Sister Rose chose to continue the tradition of wearing her white habit while at work.

Ella Randolph began her career at St. Mary's in 1966. The two pins were awarded to her on the occasion of her 5th and 15th anniversaries with the hospital.

"In those years [1960s], there was no such thing as Wite-Out. We used carbon paper and had to erase mistakes."

—Ella Randolph, secretary

Another Vatican II change allowed the nuns to return to their baptismal names. Some, like Sister Xavier, returned to their given names at this time. (Sister Xavier has been known ever since as Sister Rita Thomas.) However, Sisters Mary Monica and Rose continued using the names they had been given when they took their vows.

In the first decade of St. Mary's operation, about fourteen sisters lived in the seventh-floor convent. Few people had the occasion to glimpse that floor, although guests did come for dinner now and then, and whenever the weather prevented any of the nurses from getting home, they were offered a room in the convent. "I spent many nights in the convent," recalls Idamae Claiborne, who began work as a nursing assistant when the hospital opened. "One time when it snowed and I couldn't get home to Goochland, I stayed up there three or four nights."

"The nuns loved parties," remembers Jeanne Orr, a nurse who assisted Sister Rita, "especially in the evenings after the day was over. We had lots of parties when we opened. At first, none of us knew how to behave with the nuns. They were new to Richmond, and some people were afraid of them and didn't know how to talk to them. But they were a great group to work for." Ella Randolph, then secretary to Sister Rita, the director of nursing, remembers the annual holiday party in the convent. "It was a small hospital back then. Everybody knew everybody, like a family." Jean Grogan, a nurse in the coronary care unit, remembers, "When times were slow, the nuns kept our hands busy teaching us knitting and crocheting, but only when chores were done. And at Christmas, we sang carols on the halls. From floor to floor we went, picking up more singers from each floor."

Sister Rita led the hospital during a time of enormous growth. In short order, an ICU unit opened, a coronary care unit opened, and in 1970, the large west wing opened, doubling the hospital's size, expanding the emergency and radiology departments and adding a cobalt therapy unit. The shell for the west wing had been built during the original construction, but now that it was finished, the number of beds grew from 160 to 350, including 26 in a mental health unit. At the time of the west wing addition, the hospital had been in business four and a half years and had already cared for more than 40,000 patients.

"We were really a very progressive hospital," says Mary Ruth DeForest, who began in 1966 as assistant director of medical records under Sister Mary Monica and then became the director when her boss retired in 1979. "It was a very rewarding job. We established that department from scratch, and I was able to put into practice what I'd learned at school. We had the latest in equipment and good managers. People from other hospitals called us all the time wanting to know about our processes and procedures. People used St. Mary's as a benchmark for best practices. It was a real family atmosphere, we all knew each other and all had the same goals, so it was easy to solve problems and work together," she says.

"The presence of the sisters set the tone. Mother Germanus was very quiet, very fair, a strong leader in her own quiet way. She had a lot of respect from the medical staff. And I adored Sister Rita. She ran a tight ship and could hold her own with anyone. She was a lot of fun—at events, she'd do the polka! Sister Mary Monica was a feisty, headstrong Irish lady, feared and loved by everyone. She was the icon of St. Mary's. She saw things that needed to be done or fixed and she would march up to that person and demand it be done. She established rules for medical records and really enforced them. St. Mary's was the first hospital in the city to suspend physicians for not completing their records—physicians couldn't believe it at first!"

Noted in Volume 1, Number 1 of the 1966 St. Mary's newsletter: "True facts not worth knowing: There are over 900 doors in our building."

As the first fully integrated hospital in Richmond, St. Mary's experienced fewer racial problems than some had anticipated. Sister Rita, responsible for recruiting nurses, says, "I made a point of hiring people from the black community. My first secretary, Ella Randolph, was a black woman." She appointed a black RN, Rosalee Wilson, to be a supervisor over white nurses. No one voiced any objections. "I only remember one incident when a white patient complained about having a black woman in the same room. I told her it was our policy and that she could go elsewhere if she wanted."

"I was never conscious of any racial tensions," says Sister Rose Marie Jasinski. "I was more conscious of people thinking of me as a Yankee! I was from Baltimore, and I'd never thought of myself as a Yankee."

Dr. Stanley Goldman came to St. Mary's from the air force and university medical centers, so it was

The nursing staff is St. Mary's greatest treasure. From the left in 2001 are Barb Peek, Patti McGarry, Phyllis Brunson-Jenkins, Laura Persanowski, Bernie Smith, Judy Wyatt, and Beth Powers.

"One April Fool's Day, we played a trick on the incoming nursing team, exaggerating the numbers on our floor, telling them that so many patients had been admitted that we had to put men and women in the same room, and saying there were dozens of cardiac arrests. We really had them going!"

—Beverly Beck, former RN
and nursing instructor

Director of Pharmacy Roger Neathawk and nurse Theresa Curley Kerner meet in the hospital's pharmacy, originally located on the ground floor, to discuss a patient's requirements. St. Mary's opened with a pharmacy operation that provided in-patient medication but had no outpatient, public drug store as it does today.

his first experience at a private Catholic hospital. "It was new and quiet and clean and friendly. The staff was very welcoming, especially the sisters. There was little noise—no paging system. You picked up a pager at the desk and it beeped if you were needed while in the building. Covert discrimination existed in the small private hospitals, but there was nothing like that at St. Mary's. There were so many Jewish doctors and patients, it looked like a Jewish hospital! And the sisters couldn't have been more open and curious about other peoples' beliefs." Dr. Goldman was an

occasional dinner guest at the seventh-floor convent where he enjoyed the wide-ranging discussions. Sister Rita remembers those friendships as well. "Some of my best friends are Jewish doctors. There was mutual respect between us."

Bon Secours has always taken its role in educating healthcare professionals seriously. Mother Germanus approached the Henrico County Public Schools with an offer to co-sponsor a school of practical nursing for high school seniors. The school began in 1966 and was housed entirely at the hospital for six years until it moved to both Hermitage Technical Center and Highland Springs Technical Center. Associate degree of nursing programs started with John Tyler Community College in Chester in 1968 and at J. Sargeant Reynolds Community College in Richmond in 1973. Both colleges have used St. Mary's as a student clinical site ever since. Bon Secours also operates a separate College of Nursing, located off Parham Road, where they offer a Bachelor of Science in Nursing degree.

"Early in the practical nursing program, everything was done at St. Mary's," says Beverly Beck, an RN who taught in the original school at St. Mary's. "Classes were held in a classroom on the first floor and in a lab. Students did their clinical work with patients." These were high school students who split their days between school and hospital. "We had thirty or forty students each semester. When they graduated at eighteen, they still had to pass the licensing exam to be an LPN [licensed practical nurse], but they came out well trained. Most worked for St. Mary's when they finished, because they were familiar with the hospital, and we were familiar with them." The program continues to this day under the joint auspices of Henrico County Public Schools and St. Mary's Hospital and is now open to both high school students and adults.

In the sixties, nursing was becoming increasingly specialized, with individuals concentrating in areas such as intensive care, pediatrics, coronary care, obstetrics, and the emergency room. Team nursing

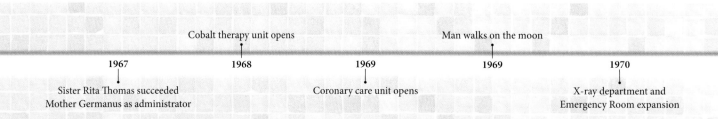

Cobalt therapy unit opens

Man walks on the moon

1967   1968   1969   1969   1970

Sister Rita Thomas succeeded
Mother Germanus as administrator

Coronary care unit opens

X-ray department and
Emergency Room expansion

WHAT IS MEANT BY A "TRAINED NURSE"

She must possess some knowledge of Elementary Anatomy and Physiology. She must understand the best methods of keeping a ward or sickroom clean and healthy, by sweeping, dusting, polishing, ventilating, warming, etc. She must understand the various methods of making a bed for medical and surgical cases, and of changing sheets, etc. She must know the best and least exhausting way of keeping a patient in a cleanly condition, and how to prevent or dress a bed sore. She must be skillful in undressing sick and injured persons, and must be able to bandage, pad splints, etc., and prepare and apply all dressings. She must know how to prepare and apply all poultices, fomentations, hot bags and bottles, blisters, lotions, leeches, ice bags, evaporating lotions, and wet packs, and prepare for cupping. Also how to give baths, hot, cold, hot air, and vapor, as regulated by the thermometer. She must understand the use of the clinical thermometer, and how to keep a chart, and record the rate of the pulse and respirations correctly. She must know the various ways of administering food, medicine, and stimulants, and know by heart the tables of weights and measures. She must be able to use quickly and correctly the various syringes and female catheters and must know the quantities generally given in enemata and injections of all kinds. She must have practical knowledge of the various systems of disinfecting patient's clothes and rooms, and keeping utensils and instruments thoroughly clean. She should possess some knowledge of cooking for the sick, and how to prepare beef-tea and jelly, chicken and mutton broth, arrow-root, cocoa, whey, egg-flip and milk puddings and also has to peptonise food.

— an article in *Trained Nurse,* December 1889

was the watchword of the decade. A registered nurse served as the team leader, supervising other RNs, LPNs, and nursing assistants. She—in those years, it was always a female—transitioned from the previous shift, scheduled X-rays, lab work, physical therapy, and other services, received new admissions, planned discharges, and arranged continuing education for the unit nursing teams.

Beck, a graduate of the University of Virginia, remembers, "It was textbook team nursing. For a graduate of a nursing program, it was exactly what you were taught at the highest level. The equipment and supplies were state-of-the-art. It was the best situation a graduate nurse could have. Because part of the purpose was learning, there were daily team conferences, a thirty-minute session where unit personnel and other hospital staff, such as physical therapists and pharmacists, would participate in a conference regarding a particular patient, disease, procedure, or other patient-care issue."

In addition to its training programs for nurses, St. Mary's introduced a two-year program to train X-ray technicians. Susanne Duff graduated with the

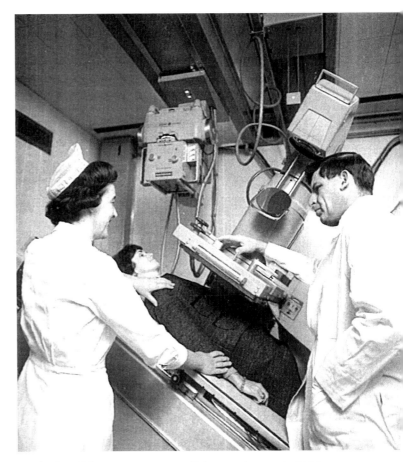

Medical staff demonstrates new radiology equipment in 1966.

Sister Elaine Davia, left, and Sister Rose O'Brien discuss the Health Wagon program.

first class in 1973. "Eight of us started the certificate program right out of high school; five graduated. I wanted to go into the medical field, but I wasn't cut out for nursing. Back then, the X-ray tech job involved heavy equipment and hand-developing in the operating room. It was different every day. You weren't stuck sitting at a desk. You touched people's lives. Now everything's digital, on computers. Now you need a college degree before X-ray school. I remember I earned $3.25 an hour, right out of school, when I'd been getting $1.75 at Thalhimers." She has worked at St. Mary's ever since, growing as the job changed. "I've always liked the people I've worked with. It's a family-oriented work environment."

Bon Secours' founding mission emphasized service to the poor, so it was natural that one of the first projects undertaken by St. Mary's Hospital was an outreach program to a remote and underserved community, reached by a mobile clinic called the Health Wagon. Sister Rita invited Sister Elaine Davia, a new sister, to come to St. Mary's and take charge of the Health Wagon.

Sister Elaine's first contact with Bon Secours had come in 1964 when she was a teenager considering

taking vows. "I knew that Bon Secours was a nursing community, so I went to Richmond to visit Mother Germanus and see what it was all about. Mother Germanus was very down-to-earth. She gave a big picnic in the backyard of the house where the nuns were living, and she included my family. That helped my parents realize that joining the order would be a human experience. In 1973, I moved to Virginia to take a family nurse practitioner course—it was a new idea then—and when I'd finished, Sister Rita asked if I would work on the home Health Wagon." It was a perfect fit for a nurse practitioner who had always wanted to work in home healthcare. "I'd been given so much in life; I wanted to give something back."

Sister Elaine recalls the original Health Wagon. "The program was not just about delivering medical care, but also about determining what was causing the health problems." The sisters had discovered a remote community in rural western Henrico County known as Francistown, where 125 families lived in shanties, many with no running water, telephones, or electricity. There was no public transportation and no way to access medical care. The hospital purchased a Dodge Sportsman wagon, furnished it with the necessary medical equipment, and sent it out four or five days a week to Francistown and other underserved rural communities, inoculating children, treating the ill and injured, providing information on good health practices. They worked to overcome the root causes of the health problems by bringing water and electricity into the homes and teaching about nutritious cooking and basic hygiene. In doing this, they were following in the footsteps of the first Bon Secours sisters in Paris.

Driving the cumbersome vehicle was the hardest part of the job, according to Sister Elaine, who found shifting gears a real challenge. "Once she backed it into a doctor's Porsche," confided one of the doctors.

In 1970, Bon Secours split the positions of religious superior and hospital administrator. Sister Elizabeth Durney was appointed superior and Sister Rita Thomas continued as hospital administrator until 1972. But the business of healthcare had become more complex and time-consuming, so the sisters decided to redirect their role to the ministry and brought in lay administrators to manage St. Mary's. At Sister Rita's suggestion, Richard D. O'Hallaron became the hospital's first lay administrator. He served for fifteen years.

NOT MANY HOSPITALS HAVE THEIR OWN ORCHESTRA

During a coffee break in the summer of 1966, Dr. Frank Sasser and Sister Mary Gemma were chatting about the fun they had playing music years before. Others chimed in, and in no time, St. Mary's had a hospital orchestra. "Some of us hadn't played in twenty years," Dr. Sasser told a reporter in 1968. "But we didn't care. The idea was to have fun and play music together." Sister Thomasine, a Trinitarian sister, served as the first conductor. "I listened to them, and they were terrible," she said, "but they had something — an enthusiasm, a love for music, and a willingness to work together." Concerts were held several times a year into the early 1980s.

SISTER RITA THOMAS (SISTER XAVIER) (1920–)

Rita Thomas grew up with her parents, Elias and Ada Thomas, two sisters, and a brother in Baltimore. She attended St. Martin's High School where one of her teachers was a young priest who would become Bishop John J. Russell of Richmond. She first met the Sisters of Bon Secours when she volunteered as a Guild Girl at the Baltimore hospital. "I felt a call to religious life," she recalls, entered the Sisters of Bon Secours in 1943, and made her perpetual profession of vows in 1951. On that occasion, she was given the name Sister Xavier, a name she used until Vatican II allowed nuns to keep their baptismal names if they preferred.

Sr. Rita earned a nursing degree from the Baltimore Bon Secours Hospital School of Nursing, a bachelor's degree from Mercy College in Detroit, and a master's degree in nursing administration from Catholic University in Washington, DC. Most of her clinical work was in obstetrics. She worked in Darby, PA, and Grosse Pointe, MI, before coming to Richmond in 1964. She opened St. Mary's Hospital as director of nursing services, recruiting and training nurses. When Mother Germanus was reassigned in 1967, Sr. Rita accepted responsibility as the hospital's second administrator, a job she performed ably until, at her urging, the first lay administrator was hired in 1972. Sr. Rita left St. Mary's for Marriottsville in 1973 to serve the Sisters of Bon Secours as Provincial Superior—the first United States Provincial elected to this leadership position. She would go on to minister in Miami before her current ministry of 35 years in Portsmouth, VA, at Maryview Medical Center. Sr. Rita's spirit and boundless energy have been recognized with local, regional, and national awards over the years. She has an eye for beauty, a creative mind, and a great love of Maryland crabs, dogs, and music as reflected in her fondness for dancing and the piano.

SISTER ROSE MARIE JASINSKI (1942–)

Sister Rose Marie Jasinski joined the Congregation of Bon Secours at the advanced age of 23. "I entered the community as an older woman," she recalls with a smile. "Most of the young women were just out of high school. I'd thought about religious life in high school. I'd always wanted to be a nurse, and I volunteered as a Pinky at the hospital." She went to the Bon Secours nursing school in Baltimore, became a registered nurse, and then joined Bon Secours.

She came to St. Mary's in 1970 at the invitation of Sister Rita, who asked her to come finish her bachelors of nursing at VCU. "St. Mary's had a very homelike atmosphere," she said. "I have so many fond memories! I got to know most of the surgeons well—they could be particular and demanding but always in context of wanting the best for the patient. I remember Dr. Knaysi's first day—he walked into the nurses' station with his white sneakers over his shoulder and he looked so young, we wondered if he was really a doctor!"

Sister Rose Marie demonstrated leadership qualities from the start. She served as head nurse at St. Mary's for a number of years and today is the leader of all Bon Secours sisters in the United States. "St. Mary's was the place where I grew up professionally."

✦ Expansion ✦

Sister Rita Thomas left St. Mary's in 1973 for her next assignment as the leader of all Bon Secours sisters in the United States. "I used to think I'd never like another place as much as St. Mary's," she recalls. "I saw it from the ground up. It was a tough time, an exciting time, to be a part of something new." She remained on the St. Mary's board of directors for many years.

Dick O'Hallaron brought his family to Richmond from St. Louis to take on the job of administrator, now called "executive director." Previous experience at two Catholic hospitals gave him more than a passing familiarity with the not-for-profit, mission-driven, healthcare model. "A Catholic hospital," he wrote, "is many people—Catholics, Protestants, Jews, and people of no acknowledged religion—working together toward common goals: the preservation of life, helping and comforting the dying, speaking out to promote the sanctity of life and finding new and improved ways to give spiritual, physical, and mental assistance to…persons of any race, creed, or financial status."

O'Hallaron was impressed with what he found at St. Mary's. "Sister Rita had assembled a group of the nicest people you'd ever want to work with. The hospital had a culture that was outstanding and highly patient-oriented, and I attribute that to Sister Rita."

His years at the helm saw tremendous growth at St. Mary's. What would turn out to be the first of three doctors' office buildings opened in 1976 as part of an extensive renovation that included moving the main entrance to the opposite side of the hospital. The wide corridor that connected the six-story, eight-million-dollar office building to the hospital also functioned as the hospital's relocated entrance. An innovative moving sidewalk carried (and continues to carry) people from the street level into the hospital lobby.

"No margin, no mission."
—oft-repeated bit of common sense

Richard O'Hallaron was the hospital's third administrator and its first lay administrator. He served from 1972-87.

When the Medical Office Building, left, opened in 1976, the hospital's main entrance shifted to a covered connector with a moving sidewalk, above.

Volunteer service to St. Mary's is often a family affair, a legacy passed down the generations. Mr. and Mrs. William B. Thalhimer, Jr., above, were donors and long-time community volunteers who had a special relationship with the hospital. Bill Jr. served on both the founding board and the foundation board. Their son, William B. Thalhimer, III, and their daughter, Barbara Thalhimer, below, have continued the family tradition.

The idea for an on-campus medical office building was new—to Richmond, at least. "Shortly after St. Mary's opened," recalls Sister Rita, "we saw the need to build a doctors' office building. I tried to convince the board that it was important. Mayor Crowe couldn't think why we needed one, but Bill Thalhimer and Mr. Muldowney on the board were very supportive." Dr. Tommy Davis and Dr. Eddy Pizzani were among the first to rent office space. Dr. Pizzani remembers, "O'Hallaron rented the building from top to bottom, and it filled up quickly. We were on the fourth floor with a great view. It was a good deal. We were practically inside the hospital. We loved being at the best hospital in Richmond." Patients appreciated the convenience of the pharmacy on the ground floor. Demand was so great that six years later, two additional floors were added.

The rapid changes occurring in modern medicine required constant updating to keep both hospital and staff on the cutting edge. "During the early 1970s," says Dr. Read McGehee, "there were significant changes in the way acute-care medicine was practiced. In a period of about five years, we got lots of new equipment, new ventilators, and we started using fiber-optic flexible scopes. The ICU was enlarged. Now we have a pediatric ICU, a post-surgical ICU, a post-cardiac ICU, and a general ICU, but back then, it was all one." In 1975, a new echocardiogram, a phonocardiogram, a holter monitor scanner, and an ultrasound unit were purchased with funds donated by the auxiliary. An occupational therapy service

"It may come as a surprise to some that the Apostolate of the Sisters of Bon Secours … is not primarily that of providing health care. In serving the sick rather it is our mission to alleviate and give redemptive meaning to human suffering and death, and in so doing to draw persons into relationship with God our Father. This mission includes a mission to all persons with whom we come in contact. It is an overwhelming and impossible human task."

— Sister Rita Thomas, remarks at the dedication of the Medical Office Building, 1975

Sister Rose Marie Jasinski, left, served at St. Mary's for thirteen years as a staff nurse, as head nurse for surgery, and later with the home health program. Here she reviews notes with a nursing assistant in 1978.

opened. A C.A.T. scanner was installed. A cardiac catheterization lab opened in 1984 for the treatment of coronary patients. "In the early 1980s," says Dr. McGehee, "my late wife established a Human Values committee at St. Mary's to help people make decisions about life and death. This reflected the changes that were occurring in treatment and medical ethics, due to all the equipment being developed that could keep people alive. St. Mary's was in the vanguard on that issue."

Outreach programs proliferated. When St. Mary's discovered a section of Amelia County that had no doctor, they built a satellite office and staffed it with a general practice physician. The Health Wagon expanded its service to rural Short Pump and Montpelier. The hospital's seven classrooms saw regular use as nurses conducted classes for expectant parents in Lamaze childbirth technique and new-born care. Husbands were now encouraged to stay with their wives in the delivery room, where more than 3,000 babies came into the world each year. The

dietary department began supplying nutritious meals to the elderly through the Meals on Wheels program. A treatment center for chemical dependency and substance abuse was established in 1980 at St. John's Hospital on River Road in Goochland County.

Sister Rose Marie Jasinski started the Home Health Service in 1979 to provide convenient, economical treatment for patients in their own homes. "One of my dreams had always been to work in home health," she remembers. "It was the holistic approach that appealed so much to me; it goes back to Bon Secours' roots in Paris, caring for people in their own homes with healthcare and also emotional care, spiritual care, and household management. St. Mary's didn't have that at the time, so I worked for a year with the Visiting Nurse Association for experience, then set up a home health program at St. Mary's and worked there as a staff nurse. Most of my home care was in the east end of Richmond in poor neighborhoods. It was a wonderful, rewarding experience."

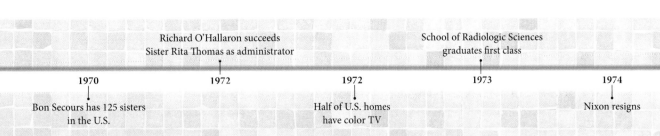

Richard O'Halloron succeeds
Sister Rita Thomas as administrator

School of Radiologic Sciences
graduates first class

| 1970 | 1972 | 1972 | 1973 | 1974 |

Bon Secours has 125 sisters
in the U.S.

Half of U.S. homes
have color TV

Nixon resigns

Sr. Elizabeth Durney founded the Bon Secours Chez Vous program at St. Mary's Hospital, where she and volunteers visit the well-elderly in their homes.

CARING

At St. Mary's, it's not just our job, it's our life's mission. The Sisters of Bon Secours at St. Mary's. They're providing spiritual support for patients. And nursing them back to health. Keeping the hospital running smoothly. And reaching out into the community. They're all an active part of a mission of caring that started over 150 years ago. When you meet a St. Mary's sister, you'll know her by the crucifix she wears. And the wonderful things she does every day. St. Mary's Hospital. A Bon Secours Health Care Facility.

ST. MARY'S HOSPITAL
Heaven Knows We Care

Sister Elizabeth Durney, above, pioneered hospice care in Richmond. Sister Vicky Segura, a hospice physician, below, was instrumental in building Richmond's first hospice house for in-patients in 2015.

"It was Sister Elizabeth Durney who introduced me to the word 'hospice' and the concept. She introduced hospice care to Richmond. Once, when the wife of a friend of mine was dying of cancer, Sister Elizabeth helped her and her husband through the dying process. Later, when Sister Elizabeth herself became ill with cancer, the husband returned to Richmond to stay with her as she died."

— Dr. Don Seitz

"St. Mary's takes risks to innovate," Sister Rose Marie says with approval, and as an example, she tells the story of the late Sister Elizabeth Durney's pioneering work in hospice care. "Sister Elizabeth had a passion for pastoral care around the dying. She had taken courses in dying, but hospice care was a new idea then. No one talked about it, and it was hard to convince people of the benefits." But as Sister Pat Eck says, "Where the sisters have gone to minister, the organization follows." Sister Elizabeth persevered, and the first rooms for hospice patients opened in 1983 with ten beds for patients who couldn't be cared for at home. "But about 95 percent of patients were cared for in their homes," says Dick O'Hallaron. Sister Jean Aulenback was one of those who nursed the dying. "It was a great program then, and it gets better all the time. I very much enjoyed working with the patients and their families in their homes." After Sister Elizabeth died at St. Mary's in 1999, her work continued under the direction of Sister Vicky Segura, a hospital and palliative care physician who shares Sister Elizabeth's passion for hospice care. In 2015, Sister Vicky led the effort to establish Richmond's first freestanding hospice facility, the Bon Secours Community Hospice House, in Chesterfield County. The mission of the Hospice House is to reduce suffering and provide comfort for terminally ill patients who cannot be cared for in their own homes.

O'Hallaron recalls another change made during his tenure as administrator. "Richmond had more for-profit hospitals at that time than any city in the United States," he said. "Those were owned by doctors, some very fine physicians, who became involved at St. Mary's, too, in leadership positions. Doctors were electing their own department chiefs who were owners of competing hospitals." To eliminate what he deemed a conflict of interest, O'Hallaron modified the bylaws of the medical staff so that the board appointed chiefs of departments—"an upsetting event, but over time, we developed a medical staff that was very loyal to St. Mary's. We started hiring full-time physicians to manage certain departments—that was a big change."

The effort to prohibit cigarette smoking caused an uproar at the board level and with the medical staff, Sister Elaine Davia recalls. "We wanted to eliminate all smoking in patients' rooms, and take cigarettes off the cart. Some doctors threatened to quit." Sister Rose Marie, who is currently on the board of Bon Secours Richmond, adds, "It was a tough sell. It was hard to convince the medical and nursing staff that smoking wasn't healthy, but eventually [in the late 1970s] smoking was banned. And pretty early on! I'm proud of that." At first, patients and staff had to go to a designated room to smoke, but eventually the entire hospital became smoke free.

"I remember when some osteopaths wanted to join the medical staff," Sister Elaine says. "That caused a heated discussion on the board before it was approved. I thought nurse practitioners should be on the staff too, and eventually that was approved as well."

In 1975, the hospital responded to a request from Henrico County to establish procedures and facilities for the evaluation and short-term care of severely disturbed, involuntary psychiatric patients. St. Mary's built a five-bed unit next to the emergency room that could hold extremely agitated patients safely, pending

"I have great respect for the sisters. Once Philip Morris wanted to do something for Bon Secours, to donate money for a research facility—lots of money. The sisters heard their presentation and turned them down. 'Their mission is different from ours,' they said."

—Dr. George Knaysi

"When my husband Harry was in the hospital with cancer, he wanted to go home to give me a birthday party. Well, he couldn't go home, so the nurses gave me a party in his room. It made him so happy. I kissed him and thanked him for the lovely party. He smiled at me and died on my 60th birthday."

—Mary Ann Sheehan,
long-time volunteer

their hearings, yet another way the hospital could serve its community.

O'Hallaron led the drive to create a master plan for the long-term future of St. Mary's campus, bringing together all parties—community representatives, political leaders, planning experts, and medical professionals—to develop a realistic vision for the hospital. "We figured out what land we needed," he recalls, "and wrote the homeowners in the area saying that we were interested in buying their property and would pay more than market value. We got the city to close Dunham Avenue from Bremo to Libbie. We spent a lot of time in meetings with neighbors keeping them informed. One time we designed landscaped buffers that the neighbors didn't like, so they came up with their own plan, and we did it. We thought good neighbors were really important."

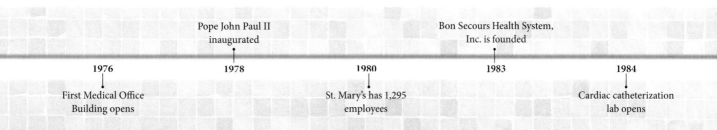

Pope John Paul II
inaugurated

Bon Secours Health System,
Inc. is founded

1976   **1978**   **1980**   **1983**   **1984**

First Medical Office
Building opens

St. Mary's has 1,295
employees

Cardiac catheterization
lab opens

Patrick Anthony Zohab, the first baby born at St. Mary's, blows out candles on the occasion of the hospital's twentieth anniversary—and his twentieth birthday—in 1986.

A birthday party marked the hospital's twentieth anniversary in 1986. Advertisements went out through the newspapers inviting all children who had been born in the hospital. *After bringing 40,000 children into the world, throwing a party for them is a piece of cake*, read the invitation. And what a cake it was—weighing in at 625 pounds! Eight thousand people showed up for the outdoor festival.

The number of sisters declined as the decade progressed, and it became apparent that the seventh-floor convent, which had been configured for as many as eighteen sisters, had more space than the eight or nine in residence could use. The hospital needed space for an ambulatory surgery unit, so in 1983, the sisters decided the logical course would be to buy a house near the hospital to use as their convent, as they had done twenty years earlier when Mother Germanus first came to Richmond. "It was a big transition," says Sister Elaine, "but a good one. However, Sister Mary Monica and Sister Rose had lived in institutional settings all their lives, and they didn't want to move out of the hospital. So the hospital kept rooms for them and made a special place for them to eat in the cafeteria. We worried about what people would say if we were to split up, but no one was surprised. It was the perfect solution." Sister Rose Marie remembers the move to the new house as a "challenge, trying to get six women to agree on carpeting and wallpaper!"

The commute by elevator was over; nonetheless, the sisters had no trouble getting to and from work each day. Security shuttled them back and forth whenever the weather made walking difficult.

During these years, hospitals became Big Business. Large corporations around the country began to buy up small hospitals, forming hospital systems that benefitted from the economies of scale. Hospital Corporation of America (HCA) came to Richmond and built Chippenham Hospital, then bought and moved Johnston-Willis to its new location south of the James River. The Medical College of Virginia (MCV) was expanding as well. When it became obvious that St. Mary's could not survive as a single, stand-alone facility, Bon Secours established its own health system in 1983, a group that would eventually include all its hospitals and health facilities throughout the United States.

"Many patients ask to go to the chapel, but we nurses can't leave the hall, so volunteers take them."

—Tiffany Wilson, RN

The hospital celebrated its 20th anniversary with a float in the Richmond Christmas Parade bearing the hospital's favorite motto of the 1980s: "Heaven Knows We Care."

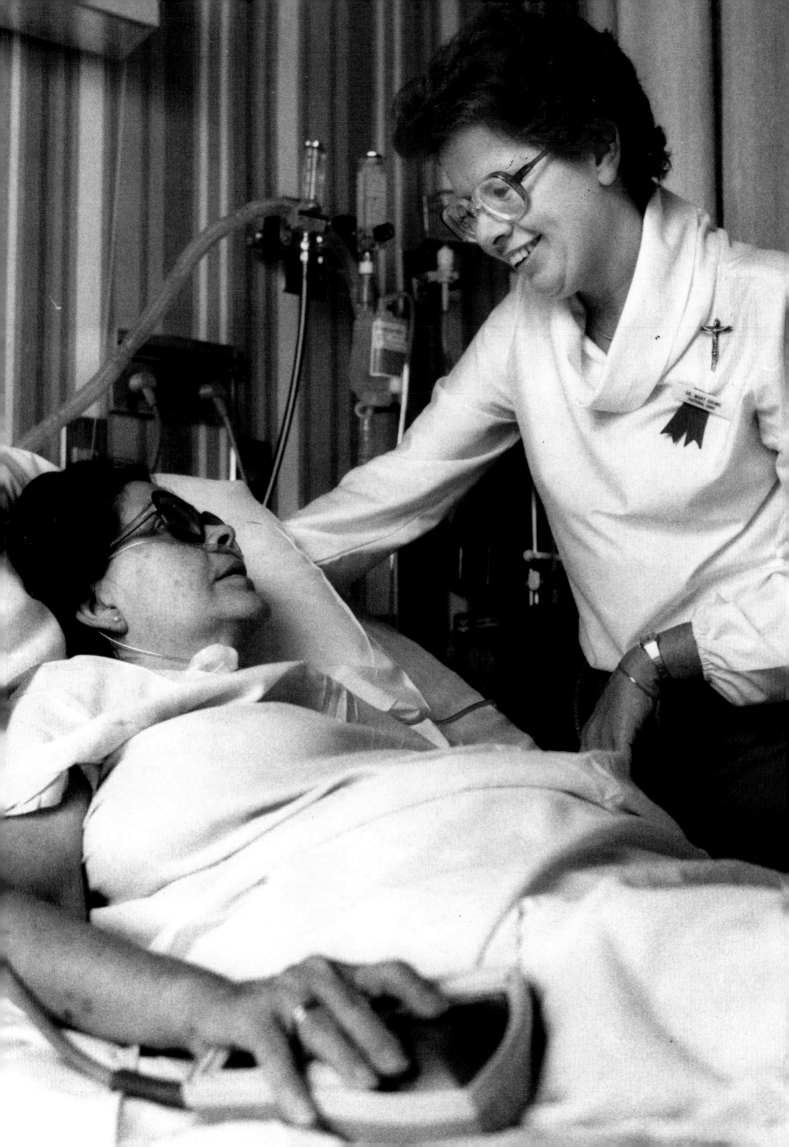

The most skilled doctors and nurses, the most modern technological wonders, and the most beautiful architecture would amount to little without the culture of compassionate care that the women of Bon Secours bring into every corner of the hospital. The spirit of the sisters—their dedication and love—permeates the building like a fragrance. "There's a special feeling when you walk in the doors of St. Mary's," says Nancy Plageman, president of the auxiliary from 1998–2000. "It's not as sterile as some. I don't know how to put it, but you know there's more than medical care here. There's comfort."

No one personified St. Mary's Hospital like Sister Mary Monica Curley. "Sister Mary Monica ruled the roost," says Dr. McGehee, and there isn't a soul alive who would disagree. "There wasn't anything she didn't know," says John Muldowney, an investment banker who served on the board, as did his father before him. Always a stickler for prompt completion of patients' records, she wouldn't let doctors admit more patients if they got behind with their medical records. Dr. Larry Zacharias remembers, "She would get after the doctors who were not keeping up their charts, and they would be censured or suspended."

"Sister Mary Monica had a desk at the top of the moving sidewalk and if you wanted to speak to her, you had to wait in line," says long-time volunteer Mary Washbourne. "She could always find a way to get things done." Ann E. Honeycutt, St. Mary's administrator from 1996–2001, remembers her

> "Sister Mary Monica would come around in the evenings and cut off lights in empty rooms to save electricity. She'd come around during the daytime to cut off all the nightlights. She did not allow her staff to wear slacks."
>
> —Earlean Didlake, unit secretary

Facing page: As St. Mary's chaplain, Sister Mary Shimo focused on pastoral care. She served at St. Mary's from 1977 to 1983.

Nancy Plageman has volunteered at St. Mary's for the past twenty-five years. "I have come to know so many wonderful people there, people I look up to."

John J. Muldowney has been a member of the hospital foundation board since the 1990s, helping to raise funds for the hospital.

A company representative demonstrates the hospital's new Lektriever filing system to Sister Mary Monica. This revolving file held about two years of medical records. When it became full, the inactive records were purged and moved to open shelving.

"On my first day, I couldn't find the operating room right away. Someone needed an appendectomy. When I finished, I went to the records room where Sister Mary Monica hung out. She was tough. I walked in and said, 'I'm here to do my records,' and she showed me the papers. When I finished, I signed them, and laid them down and started to leave. 'Young man,' she said, 'do you leave things lying around at your house?' I said no. 'Put them over there,' she said. I obeyed. Everyone obeyed Sister Mary Monica."

—Dr. George Knaysi

"sitting in the lobby, greeting people. She was very visible, always making the rounds and keeping up with the young doctors, asking if they passed their boards."

Mary Ruth DeForest started working as Sister Mary Monica's assistant when the hospital opened. "They called us medical records librarians in those days, then registered record administrators, then health information managers," she says. "After Sister Mary Monica died, they created an endowment in her name." The Sister Mary Monica "Good Samaritan" Fund helps with the medical bills for patients who are making a good-faith effort but can't afford to pay their bill.

Sister Rose O'Brien earned the distinction of having served at the hospital longer than any other sister: forty years. "She was a tiny thing," remembers Dr. McGehee, "and a terrible driver. Once she had an accident on Libbie and was in intensive care for a long time." Others use words like "angelic" and "sweet" to describe her. "Sister Rose was a quiet person," says Washbourne, "small in stature, an introvert, but you could feel her warmth and her acceptance of others. She did things in the background." From the day the hospital doors opened, Sister Rose worked in the blood bank with a calm efficiency that endeared her to everyone. Sister Elaine remembers that she had such a delicate touch, she could draw blood from frightened children or others who were fearful of the process. Sister Rose and Sister Mary Monica were the traditionalists: the two who chose to continue wearing the traditional white habit and who continued living in the hospital after the other sisters moved to their off-campus convent home on Monument Avenue.

Sister Rose helped open St. Mary's and she spent the next forty years there, supervising the pathology department and working in the lab. Beloved by all, she had a special affinity with sick children, who were calmed by her gentle manner and her skillful handling of needles. She is shown here receiving her ten-year service pin in 1976.

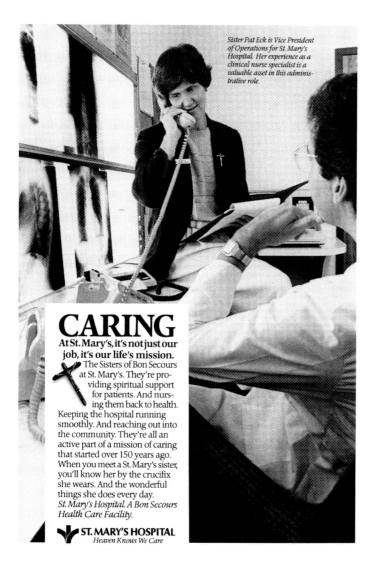

Sister Pat Eck is Vice President of Operations for St. Mary's Hospital. Her experience as a clinical nurse specialist is a valuable asset in this administrative role.

CARING

At St. Mary's, it's not just our job, it's our life's mission.

The Sisters of Bon Secours at St. Mary's. They're providing spiritual support for patients. And nursing them back to health. Keeping the hospital running smoothly. And reaching out into the community. They're all an active part of a mission of caring that started over 150 years ago. When you meet a St. Mary's sister, you'll know her by the crucifix she wears. And the wonderful things she does every day. St. Mary's Hospital. A Bon Secours Health Care Facility.

✚ ST. MARY'S HOSPITAL
Heaven Knows We Care

The story of Sister Patricia Eck is that of the local girl who became a star. "I knew Sister Pat back when we were in grade school in Richmond," says John Muldowney. "She came from a fine Catholic family—good charitable people." She joined Bon Secours in 1966 and began her career as an operating-room nurse at St. Mary's. She served in a number of supervisory positions, earned a masters degree in nursing and a masters in health administration, and became the hospital's chief operating officer before ultimately being named the leader of the entire Bon Secours international congregation. Although she lives and works today at the Bon Secours headquarters in Maryland, she considers St. Mary's her home.

"Sometimes," remembers Dr. George Knaysi, "my wife and I would be invited up to the seventh floor for dinner with the sisters, and Sister Pat and Sister Rose Marie would play the guitar and sing. In those days, there were sisters all over the hospital. It gave the place a special feeling."

Sister Jean Aulenback was assigned to St. Mary's for only four and a half years, but she made a lasting impression. Born in Nova Scotia, she came to the United States where she got a job working in a Bon Secours hospital as a registered nurse. "I had no intention of becoming Catholic and certainly no intention of becoming a nun," she says with a smile, "but I was curious. I became Catholic because I was curious! I got instruction and started inquiring about Bon Secours. I was asking myself, what do I want to do with the rest of my life?" She found the answer: she took her vows in 1958. "Bon Secours hospitals are the best because the people are so dedicated. It's not just the physical care, like giving pain medication. It's the personal attention, taking time to talk to the patient. It can be difficult sometimes, but patients often need someone to talk to. That's what the Bon Secours mission means to me: following Jesus and doing what Jesus would do for people."

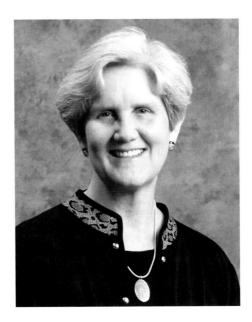

Sister Pat Eck

"When the sisters of Bon Secours first came to Richmond, I was in high school," says Sister Pat Eck. Her connection with the congregation began in the early 1960s when she helped her mother volunteer with the fund-raising bazaars. "I met Sister Frances Helen who one day asked me if I might be interested in religious life—and I said to myself, 'Stay away from that woman!'" But Sister Frances Helen must have seen something in the girl, for God was calling Pat Eck. She chose to enter Bon Secours in 1966 because of its nursing mission.

Born and raised in Richmond in a large Catholic family, she began working at St. Mary's as an operating room nurse. "I've been on and off at St. Mary's for half my professional life," she says, "and I've seen it grow from the very beginning. There were days when I left the convent on the seventh floor and went to the operating room on the ground floor and never saw light of day. Those were great times—we had a wonderful crew in OR."

"St. Mary's is the place that cares for my family: my mother died there, my brother died there, and about twenty of my grandnieces and nephews were born there. For me, it's home. I still go back to St. Mary's for some of my clinical care. I love St. Mary's."

Sister Rita, who was then hospital administrator, saw something special in Pat as well, and later when she was provincial, encouraged her to continue her education at Catholic University, where she earned a masters degree in nursing, followed by a masters in health administration at Virginia Commonwealth University. In 1985 she returned to St. Mary's as COO—"I had an incredible welcome." Today she lives and works in Marriottsville, MD, where she has been the congregation leader for the Sisters of Bon Secours of Paris since 2009, but she can often be found in Richmond at St. Mary's Hospital.

Sister Mary Monica Curley (1903–1996)

Catherine Ernestine was born on March 16, 1903, to Joseph Curley, an Irish immigrant, and his wife, Susan Riley, in Pawtucket, RI. Before discerning a vocation to religious life, Catherine worked as a secretary and occasional substitute teacher. But her heart was with the poor and the sick of her parish, and as she found herself drawn to religious life, a priest recommended her to the Sisters of Bon Secours. An automobile accident delayed but did not deter her entrance into a lifetime ministry, which formally began in 1937. Because of World War II, Sr. Mary Monica could not go in 1946 to the congregation motherhouse in Paris to affirm her final vows as was then the custom. She earned her RN from the Baltimore Bon Secours Hospital School of Nursing, then went on to complete training as an X-ray technician and records librarian. Her versatility was welcomed in Darby, PA; Baltimore, MD; Methuen, MA; and Grosse Pointe, MI, before she was appointed in 1965 to Richmond, VA, to open St. Mary's Hospital as medical record administrator and librarian. It was the third hospital she had helped to establish. While at St. Mary's, she opened the emergency and X-ray departments, established the medical records department and the health science library, and served on the hospital's board of directors. "The heart and pulse of any hospital are its medical records, and it's important we keep them at our fingertips," she often said. She celebrated her 50th year of service to the Congregation of Bon Secours in 1987 at St. Mary's Hospital chapel. For decades, Sr. Mary Monica was the personification of the hospital. She inspired so much love and affection that a fund was created at her death. The Sister Mary Monica "Good Samaritan" Fund helps patients who cannot afford medical care. Sr. Mary Monica died at the Marriottsville motherhouse and is buried in Mount Cavalry Cemetery in Richmond.

SISTER ROSE O'BRIEN (1915–2010)

Margaret O'Brien was born on March 7, 1915, in Philadelphia, PA, to Joseph and Ann Jane Taggart O'Brien. She worked at the Bon Secours home for crippled children in Philadelphia, becoming so impressed with the sisters' work and their mission that she entered the Congregation of Bon Secours in 1932—"a choice that did not make [her] father too happy." Sr. Rose of Lima professed her final vows in 1941. She earned her RN from the Baltimore Bon Secours Hospital School of Nursing in 1937 and her B.S. in medical technology from Notre Dame of Maryland in 1958. She taught pediatric nursing and microbiology, became certified in blood bank technology, and served as a medical technologist in Baltimore, MD, and Methuen, MA, before being sent in 1965 to help open St. Mary's Hospital in Richmond.

At St. Mary's, she began as supervisor of the pathology department and worked in the lab until 1991. In 1982 she celebrated her Golden Jubilee—fifty years as a sister of Bon Secours—with a special mass at St. Mary's Hospital chapel that was celebrated by her brother, Rev. Joseph O'Brien. Reflecting on her lifetime spent at the hospital, she said, "I like it very, very much. I was very happy there." She was a faithful friend to Sr. Mary Monica Curley (1903–1996) and became her advocate during her illness and death. Sr. Rose continued to share her joyfulness, her gracious smile, and her playfulness with patients and visitors alike until 2005. Then she transferred to a ministry of prayer in Marriottsville, MD, where she knew how to make, serve, and enjoy a proper cup of tea. Her faithfulness, single-mindedness, and persistence kept her moving and ministering as a Sister of Bon Secours for 78 years. She died at the Marriottsville motherhouse, but was buried in Mount Cavalry Cemetery in Richmond.

✦ From Hospital to Health System ✦

Christopher M. Carney replaced Dick O'Hallaron as St. Mary's administrator in 1987, a position Carney held for ten years. The decade saw explosive growth in Bon Secours, which, like other health systems in Virginia and across the nation, was restructuring its business model, combining individual hospitals into a network to increase efficiency and offer more services. In the space of a few years, Bon Secours acquired Stuart Circle Hospital, Richmond Memorial Hospital, and Richmond Community Hospital, forming the Bon Secours Richmond Health Corporation to manage them.

Carney had come to St. Mary's in 1981 as chief operating officer, and when he retired in 2005, it was as the CEO of all the Bon Secours hospitals and healthcare facilities in the United States. These were the years when Bon Secours began to expand from one hospital to a health system that today consists of five hospitals in the Richmond area (St. Mary's Hospital, St. Francis Medical Center, Richmond Community Hospital, Memorial Regional Medical Center, and Rappahannock General Hospital) and three in Virginia's Hampton Roads region. "We took what we'd learned at St. Mary's, and applied it to all the hospitals," Carney says, "avoiding duplication where possible. Wherever it made financial sense, we consolidated support services, like supply-chain management and various types of insurance programs." The most significant accomplishment during his tenure was the creation of those entities, as well as the Central Virginia Health Network, a consortium of not-for-profit hospitals partnering to negotiate managed care contracts and to share such services as purchasing, transportation, and advertising, which led to greater efficiency and cost savings for all.

At St. Mary's Hospital, the Carney years saw the opening of the cardiac surgery suite for open-heart

Left to right: Sister Pat Eck, Administrator Ann Honeycutt, Chris Carney, and Dr. Thomas Davis, at a 1997 meeting

"Whenever you were faced with a tough decision, you asked yourself, what would a sister of Bon Secours do?"

— Chris Carney, St. Mary's administrator 1987–1996

surgery, the neonatal intensive care unit, the first parking deck, a second medical office building, and the Care-a-Van program. This also marked the beginning of fund-raising activities through the reorganized St. Mary's Hospital Foundation. A trend toward separate facilities for children led to a new pediatric intensive care unit in 1989, where doctors treated 130 young patients in its first year of operation. A pediatric emergency room opened six years later and today treats more than 23,000 young patients annually. Bursting at the seams, St. Mary's gained some breathing space with the south wing, a five-story building completed in 1992 that housed a new emergency department, birthing center, medical laboratory, and an expanded surgery suite. "All the

Facing page: The second Medical Office Building (South) opened in 1992. Three floors were added in 2000, along with a new emergency entrance that expanded again in 2012, as pictured here, when a separate pediatric emergency department was established.

"St. Mary's has been a catalyst in Richmond, reaching out into the community to provide health."

—Chris Carney, St. Mary's administrator 1987–1996

new office buildings magnified the need for more parking," recalls Carney. Limited acreage dictated the solution: a parking deck. Later that deck more than doubled in size.

The Care-a-Van program began in 1994 with a lot of publicity, but it was actually a continuation of the previous Health Wagon ministry. "It was a perfect vehicle to bring services to the community," says Carney, acknowledging the pun. "It fit with the sisters' mission, since bringing care to the home was how they were founded." The program was so successful, it spread throughout Virginia, growing to five Care-a-vans plus a multitude of other vehicles designed to provide care, health education, and wellness services to underserved areas. Today the Care-a-vans serve more than 20,000 people annually.

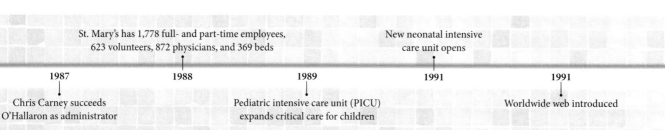

St. Mary's has 1,778 full- and part-time employees, 623 volunteers, 872 physicians, and 369 beds

New neonatal intensive care unit opens

1987	1988	1989	1991	1991
Chris Carney succeeds O'Hallaron as administrator		Pediatric intensive care unit (PICU) expands critical care for children		Worldwide web introduced

Bon Secours' commitment to its patients and to the community had become well known throughout central Virginia, but just as important was its commitment to its employees, whose numbers had grown from 350 to 1,800 in less than twenty-five years. The hospital consistently ranked at the top of the *Working Mother* Best Places to Work list. In opening its Family Center in 1989, the hospital provided its employees with convenient, high-quality daycare for their children. Family Center Director Donna Shifflett explains that the center operates on a schedule that accommodates hospital employees' long hours and is open Mondays through Saturdays. "We serve more than two hundred families, including our summer camp and school holiday camps for school-aged children. The Family Center's census averages 90 to 100 infants and children each day." She notes with pride that many of the center's children, now grown, are employed at St. Mary's Hospital and other Bon Secours facilities.

Chris Carney acknowledged the many improvements in clinical services and additions

In 1988, St. Mary's opened its Child Care Center on the campus to give employees a safe and convenient place for their children.

Bon Secours' advertising agency hired several youngsters, all experienced models, to advertise Health Day 1986. One was **Tiffany Wilson**, who happened to have been born at St. Mary's eight years earlier. When her mother took her to Health Day, the nurses there made a big impression on the child. "I saw the nurses doing blood pressure and other tests," she remembers, "and it looked like such fun that I made up my mind to become a nurse when I grew up." After graduating from George Mason University, she came home to attend Bon Secours' nursing school. Since 2005, she has worked at St. Mary's on the sixth floor as an oncology nurse, sometimes in charge of the floor, sometimes as a staff nurse. "I was attracted by the idea of taking care of people, of putting others before self. Oncology has a lot of end-of-life patients, so it can be sad, but it's rewarding. You're there for the family."

Sister Elizabeth Durney discusses a patient's care with a nurse.

to the physical facilities that took place during his tenure at St. Mary's. "Growth, expansion, and change are expected in the ever-changing healthcare landscape," says Carney. "What has remained constant is the mission of the sisters. What they established for St. Mary's and Richmond is what sets us apart from other hospitals and healthcare entities. Our calling—good help to those in need—is rooted in compassion and spiritual healing of mind, body, and spirit. It's a philosophy unique to Bon Secours."

The Bon Secours presence in Richmond continued to expand. When the Bon Secours Health System purchased Stuart Circle Hospital, built in 1918 in the Fan District, it allowed them to consider closing the old building and moving those hospital beds to a new facility in Chesterfield County where the need was greater. Eventually, they opened St. Francis Medical Center in Midlothian. Ann Honeycutt, CEO of Stuart Circle Hospital at that time, recalls, "The sisters leveraged their success at St. Mary's to spread their mission across Richmond by partnering with or purchasing other hospitals. They filled the gaps in services for residents in many areas of greater Richmond." Honeycutt was named administrator of St. Mary's in 1996, and until Stuart Circle closed, remained responsible for both. "My focus was on broadening St. Mary's reach in the community.

"From the start, St. Mary's mission was different from other hospitals. The patient came first, not profits. Its costs were significantly less than other hospitals. The mission of the Sisters of Bon Secours has always had a major impact on strategic decisions and employee decisions."

—Ann E. Honeycutt, administrator 1996–2001

The Environmental Services staff in 2000 included, from left to right, Eleanor Carter, Preston Lane, Amelia Bynum, Angelo Jones, Jeanette Watkins, and Donald Jackson.

During my tenure, we opened Memorial Regional Medical Center [formerly Richmond Memorial Hospital] in Hanover County and added Richmond Community Hospital in Church Hill to the Bon Secours family. One of my goals was to make sure St. Mary's remained stable and continued to grow." Her efforts paid off. "We added a new wing onto the fourth floor with private rooms, worked hard to build our obstetric business, expanded emergency services, and added five new operating rooms and three floors to the South Medical Office building, making room for additional physician practices."

Ralph Wheeler, administrative director of engineering, security and safety, and Carolyn Bohannon, administrative secretary, have worked together for nineteen years.

Care-a-Van program begins

Ann Honeycutt succeeds
Carney as administrator

1992   1994   1995   1996   2000

South Wing, parking deck, and second
Medical Office Building open

Pediatric emergency
room opens

Human genome sequence
deciphered

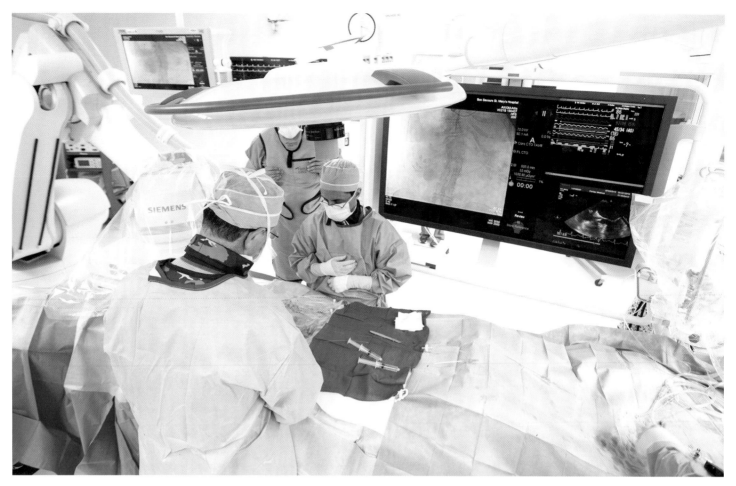

Scott Lim, MD, and Marc Katz, MD, perform a procedure in 2015 using the latest technology in transcatheter aortic valve implantation (TAVI). The Evolut-R tool allows for excellent outcomes for the most difficult cardiovascular cases.

In 1994, the MEDACOM–Virginia electronic communications network allowed doctors to communicate instantly with network hospitals and other physicians, promoting increased efficiency in patient care.

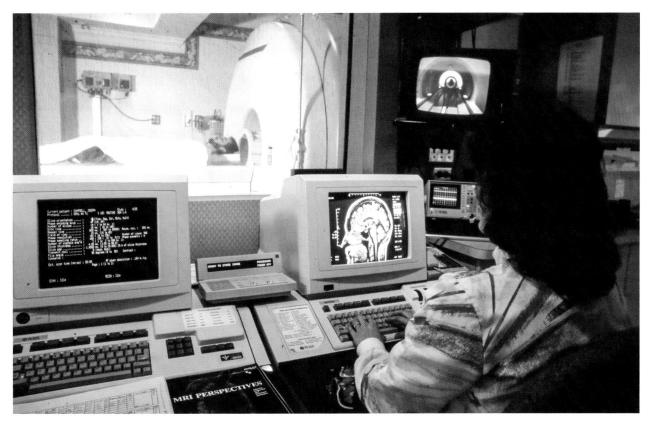

St. Mary's has always been a leader in health care technology, providing magnetic resonance imaging (MRI), CT Scan, mammography, and other services, as shown in this 1994 photo.

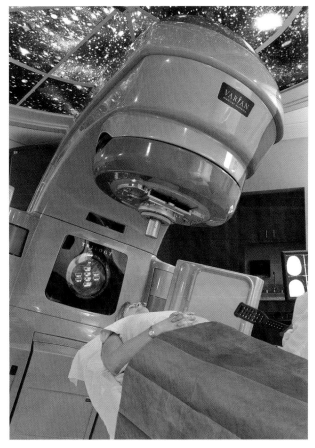

The first spine robotics surgery was performed at St. Mary's in 2013. The surgical team uses the latest equipment to transform spine surgery from freehand operations to highly accurate, state-of-the-art procedures. This minimally invasive technique lowers complications and reduces postoperative pain.

Clinicians at St. Mary's use the latest in advanced radiotherapy to deliver a wide range of cancer treatments every day, shortening patient treatment times and minimizing damage to healthy tissues.

ichael Kerner came to St. Mary's from HCA in 2001, but this new administrator was not new to Richmond or unfamiliar with St. Mary's. There already existed a family connection. "My mother was a nurse at St. Mary's, my aunt worked in the recovery room, and my uncle volunteered here. Also, my brother was born at St. Mary's and several other relatives were cared for here," he says.

"I had been in healthcare for many years at about eight different hospitals before coming to St. Mary's. The community support at St. Mary's was the strongest I've ever seen. I believe it comes from our community involvement and outreach. We touch so many through a variety of channels. We have a Community Advisory board made up of volunteer leadership and the governing boards for all Richmond hospitals; we have an auxiliary board… More than one hundred people are serving on various hospital boards, creating support and momentum for our ministry." Another very special aspect of St. Mary's is its strong volunteer base. "They are by far the largest and most engaged volunteer group I've ever worked with," said Kerner. "They are committed to our ministry and are wonderful representatives for us, often the first people our visitors encounter and the last they see before they go home."

During the Kerner administration, three floors were built atop the hospital's south tower, significantly raising the number of private rooms and adding orthopedic beds. The neonatal intensive care unit was upgraded and expanded, the mother/infant unit grew, and a new medical office building—the third on campus—was constructed with an ambulatory surgery center for outpatients. "During my time, the number of physicians grew significantly," he says, "especially pediatric specialties and subspecialties, and we increased the number of physician employees."

Michael Kerner began his Bon Secours career at St. Mary's in 2001. Today he is CEO of Bon Secours Hampton Roads Health System.

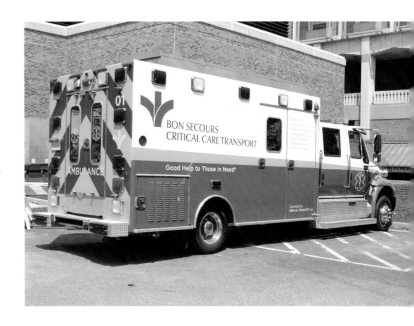

The dietary staff poses for a photo in 2001.

Nathan Hill and Carolyn Bohannon from security enjoy a break in the coffee shop in 2001.

Sister Anne Marie Mack came to St. Mary's during the Kerner administration as vice president of mission and has been in Richmond ever since. "I got to know the sisters very well as a high school student in Darby, PA," she says, "working as a nurse's aid at a Bon Secours nursing home after school and on weekends. It was my first experience with sisters who were nurses—previously, all the nuns I knew were teachers at my Catholic school. The Bon Secours sisters were so down-to-earth and such a lot of fun; I learned so much from them." She joined Bon Secours after finishing high school in 1965. After three years of training as a postulant, she attended the University of Delaware where she earned a bachelor's degree in nursing and then began her career at Bon Secours hospitals in Baltimore and Michigan. Later, she was elected "Provincial," leading all the Bon Secours sisters in the United States, a position that lasted for eight years. In 2007, she began her work at St. Mary's. After serving as

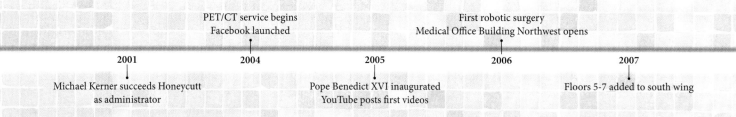

PET/CT service begins
Facebook launched

First robotic surgery
Medical Office Building Northwest opens

2001   2004   2005   2006   2007

Michael Kerner succeeds Honeycutt
as administrator

Pope Benedict XVI inaugurated
YouTube posts first videos

Floors 5-7 added to south wing

St. Mary's vice president of mission, she was promoted to senior vice president of sponsorship, where she partnered with Bon Secours Richmond's CEO Peter Bernard, governing all Bon Secours operations in greater Richmond (and eventually all of Virginia) with oversight of mission activities. "What impresses me most about St. Mary's is the level of commitment our employees have with regard to the mission and values of Bon Secours. They embrace our culture and act as any sister of Bon Secours would. That makes me so proud."

As the years progressed, the number of sisters working at St. Mary's declined. "There were several sisters here when I arrived," says Kerner. "Sister Rose was in the lab, still wearing her habit; Sister Anne Marie was a strong proponent of our Catholic identity; Sister Frances Helen spent much of her time talking with patients, advocating for them and ministering to them; Sister Pat Eck worked in the operating room before she went into administration. Together they added a real sense of spirituality to the hospital." But it was obvious that the number of sisters and nuns was shrinking, not just in the Congregation of Bon Secours, but throughout America. The year St. Mary's Hospital opened, there were 181,431 Catholic religious women in the United States; today, there are fewer than 50,000. According to Father Giancarlo Rocca, a scholar of the history of religious orders, factors contributing to the decline include secularism, the anti-authority movement of the 1960s, and the shrinking of Catholic family size, but "the key is the emancipation of women. Previously, the socially approved options for women were either to marry and have children or join a religious order."

"We were all aware of the trend," says Kerner, "and we began planning for the future, passing the torch to lay people who could carry on the Bon Secours ministry." This mechanism is known in Catholic Church law as a *Public juridic person,* where a person (or, more typically, a group of people) is empowered by the Church to oversee the mission of an institution, ensuring that the institution is run according to Catholic principles. The group usually

"We stand on the shoulders of the sisters who came before us."
—Sister Anne Marie Mack, 2015

Sisters Mary Monica, Elizabeth, and Rose are buried in Mt. Calvary Cemetery, a Catholic cemetery located beside Richmond's historic Hollywood Cemetery.

includes a mix of religious and lay people. In the case of Bon Secours, a Ministries Board was created in 2006, with half its members lay people and half sisters. The board reports to Rome and has responsibility for all the Bon Secours operations in the United States. In this way, the mission of St. Mary's Hospital will be preserved into the future.

✦ Culture of Bon Secours ✦

 nder the leadership of Peter Bernard, Bon Secours' many hospitals and medical facilities in Virginia were growing apace. Bon Secours Richmond combined with the hospitals in the Hampton Roads region to become Bon Secours Virginia, and Michael Kerner was promoted from St. Mary's to Hampton Roads to oversee those facilities (Maryview Medical Center, Mary Immaculate Hospital, and DePaul Medical Center). Toni R. Ardabell took his place as CEO of St. Mary's.

Ardabell is the leader who prepared St. Mary's for its 50th year, taking the helm of Bon Secours' flagship hospital in 2009. All it took was one visit to the St. Mary's campus, and Ardabell knew she was home. "I knew within moments that there was something extraordinary about St. Mary's and Bon Secours, overall," said Ardabell, now CEO of Bon Secours Richmond Health System. "I could feel the culture and see the mission at work—it was evident everywhere."

A healthcare veteran and a nurse by training, Ardabell recognized that Bon Secours was unlike any hospital or healthcare system she had previously

Toni Ardabell came to St. Mary's Hospital in 2008. Today she is CEO of the Bon Secours Richmond Health System.

"People are more important to us than things. More important than bureaucracy or budget. People are not room numbers, diagnoses or statistics. They are human persons entitled to dignity and respect for their individual needs."

—statement from the Sisters of Bon Secours, 1985, *Richmond Times-Dispatch*

Bon Secours Virginia

Richmond

Bon Secours Home Health & Hospice; Bon Secours Ambulatory Services; Bon Secours Medical Group; Memorial Regional Medical Center, Mechanicsville; Rappahannock General Hospital, Kilmarnock; Richmond Community Hospital, Richmond; St. Francis Medical Center, Midlothian; St. Mary's Hospital, Richmond

Hampton Roads

Bon Secours Home Health & Hospice
Bon Secours Ambulatory Services
Bon Secours Medical Group
Depaul Medical Center, Norfolk
Mary Immaculate Hospital, Newport News
Maryview Medical Center, Portsmouth

Facing page: Two nurses enjoy their lunch break in the sunshine.

This statue of Our Lady sheltering children was hand carved in Germany for the hospital's pediatric wing.

experienced. "Nurses are inherently compassionate, but the level of compassion I witnessed—and still witness today—at every level of the organization was exemplary. There is a feeling of peacefulness at St. Mary's. I can't say whether it comes from the daily prayer broadcast or the quiet hours across the hospital each afternoon, but you have a sense that everything is going to be okay. That's important for our employees as well as our patients and visitors."

Nurturing and enhancing the culture of Bon Secours lies at the heart of Ardabell's leadership. "How we treat our patients, visitors, and one another is critical to our success as healthcare providers. Not to mention, treating everyone with respect is simply the right way to behave," says Ardabell. "Accomplishing our goals comes much more naturally when we work with respect and are open to all views."

As Ardabell reflects on St. Mary's rich history in Richmond, she talks about the significance of the hospital to the community. "Not many people today are aware that St. Mary's was not only the first faith-based hospital in Richmond, but the first integrated hospital. It is important to remember that the sisters

Peter Bernard, former CEO of Bon Secours Virginia Health System, came to Richmond at the start of the new millennium to lead the Bon Secours hospital group that included St. Mary's. He retired in 2015. Bernard's many contributions helped make Bon Secours the premier health system it is today. Under his guidance, Bon Secours became the first health system in the state to introduce electronic medical records, beginning with St. Mary's Hospital. He worked diligently to make the Bon Secours work environment, employee wellness, and employment benefits a priority. Recognizing that a strong nursing program is the backbone of any healthcare system, he provided opportunities for nurses to excel professionally. As a result, St. Mary's and two other Bon Secours Richmond hospitals achieved Magnet status, a recognition program that acknowledges high-quality patient care and nursing excellence. Other milestones include the building of St. Francis Medical Center, the establishment of St. Francis Watkins Centre, and the addition of Rappahannock General Hospital to the Bon Secours family.

A St. Mary's family: Ron and Tonya Harris met and married while they worked at the hospital, she as an administrative assistant in Respiratory Care Services and he with the surgical orthopedic team. Their daughter Ava was born at St. Mary's in 2014.

Style Weekly readers have voted St. Mary's Hospital the "Favorite Place in Richmond to Have a Baby" from 2003 to 2012 (when the survey ended).

took a stand on segregation. It changed the way healthcare was delivered in this community."

So important is the hospital's legacy that upon her arrival at St. Mary's, Ardabell established the annual Legacy Dinner for retired physicians, who gather each year to remember the early days at St. Mary's. "It is important that we draw on our past, remembering the trials and successes and the early days of the sisters in Richmond. The stories, the history, and the people form the fabric of St. Mary's and we want to carry that into 2016 and beyond."

During the Ardabell administration, the nursing team achieved Magnet status, the most prestigious recognition for nursing in the United States, and St. Mary's became one of only five community hospitals in the country with an LVAD (partial artificial heart) program, something generally reserved for transplant centers. The exceptional quality of care and the high level of patient satisfaction has propelled St. Mary's

into the upper echelons of hospital rankings in America. St. Mary's ranks among the top fifty cardiovascular hospitals in the country and the Top 100 Best Hospitals with Great Heart Programs. St. Mary's has climbed into the top 10 percent for critical care, stroke, and prostatectomy. *U.S. News* recently ranked St. Mary's as #2 in Richmond and #6 in Virginia.

"St. Mary's has been voted the best place in Richmond to have a baby for the past dozen years," adds Nellie League, who supervises 1,200 nurses at St. Mary's as chief nursing officer. "We promote a high-touch, low-tech delivery, with a one-to-one patient-to-nurse ratio to ensure that the mother has the experience *she* wants, and we go to great lengths to make that happen. In the 1990s, giving birth was a 24-hour experience; now it's two days, giving mothers time to adjust."

St. Mary's prizes its reputation as Richmond's best hospital for giving birth. Nurses, above, proudly introduce the babies born that day. Below, Bonnie Makdad, MD, a neonatologist, works with one of St. Mary's youngest and most fragile patients.

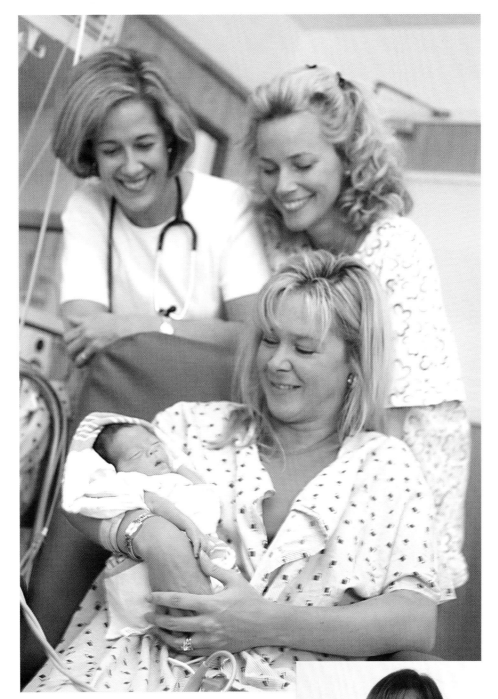

Lisa Friedkin, the mother of twin boys born prematurely, holds her son Nicholas in the neonatal intensive care unit. Dr. Bonnie Makdad and Nurse Sherry Wilson look on.

THREE GENERATIONS

St. Mary's is truly a Richmond tradition. Many families have welcomed their second or third generations into the world at St. Mary's. Nonie Redford gave birth to her daughter Halie, the mother of Colin Sanchez, born in 1998.

"Sometimes when I see the retired doctors, I recognize the face, then the name pops up, and I can visualize their handwriting. ConnectCare came in 2010 and what I could do best—reading the doctor's handwriting—was no longer important. There was no more trying to figure out what was handwritten. That made me sad. My husband, who had been sick for several years, died in 2010. I had lost two things that meant so much to me."

—Earlean Didlake,
unit secretary

Dr. George Parker, former chief of surgery, served as president of the medical staff from 2010–11.

The digital age brought sweeping changes to the practice of medicine, none more disruptive than when paper records gave way to computers. A federal effort to improve medical care and rein in costs encouraged the development and use of an electronic record-keeping system. At St. Mary's, a system known as ConnectCare was instituted in 2010. "It was a big change," says Anne Dunnington, a graduate of Bon Secours Memorial College of Nursing who has worked at St. Mary's since 2005. "ConnectCare changed the dynamic between physicians and nurses. Now physicians can put in orders, see charts, and check on patients from their home or office. The documentation is more thorough." Dr. George Parker, former chief of surgery and president of St. Mary's medical staff, says, "Although ConnectCare is not yet a perfect system, some things are far better. X-rays were a nuisance to retrieve before, and now they're right on the chart. We used to have to call the lab and ask for reports or have them faxed, which took time. Electronic records have really facilitated that. The biggest challenge now is providing seamless care between primary care physicians to the specialists to the hospital and back to the primary care physician." Dr. George Knaysi notes that St. Mary's came early to the table. "Electronic records were implemented about four or five years ago at St. Mary's. Other hospitals were behind us."

A robot joined the staff in 2013! The TRU-D Smart "droid" disinfects a room after it has been manually cleaned, using ultraviolet light to eliminate 99.99 percent of bacteria. Dr. Khiet Trinh, chief medical officer at St. Mary's, says, "Patient safety is the crux of what we do. This machine helps us give patients the safest environment possible." St. Mary's and two other Bon Secours hospitals were the first in the region to institute this new technology.

"When I came to St. Mary's in 1984," says Knaysi, "it was a quaint community hospital. Today, it still has that warm, welcoming feeling. The biggest change has been the expansion of services—caring for much sicker, high-risk patients. We don't transfer

Affordable Care Act passes

Pope Francis inaugurated

| 2009 | 2010 | 2010 | 2013 | 2015 |

Toni Ardabell succeeds Kerner as administrator

ConnectCare electronic recordkeeping launched

St. Mary's has 2,329 employees; Francine Barr succeeds Ardabell as administrator

Idamae Claiborne has worked at St. Mary's since it opened in 1966. "Some of my mother's friends in Goochland where we lived told her about a new hospital being built in Richmond. I had just completed a one-year nursing class. I was young and shy and afraid, but I got over that. I got my first job at St. Mary's. Each day I had to report on each patient on the floor. I gave baths, fed them, did lots of lifting. There was no cath lab then, and they had to go to MCV for that. After about one year on the job, I took a class to become a patient technician; learned to take blood pressure and things. Then in 1983, they [did away with] patient techs and nursing assistants, but I consider myself blessed, because I went to respiratory/EKG and trained on equipment there. I've been there ever since."

preemies any more; we have a specialized cardio-vascular intensive care unit; we have a pediatric intensive care unit, a neonatal intensive care unit, and more high-risk pregnancies. There is very little that can't be done here today. But medical care has become more complex. The velocity is so fast now. In the old days, in the summer they would close a floor to give people time off. It was not so busy. That doesn't happen any longer—the hospital is almost always full.

The role of the registered nurse has expanded as they take on greater responsibilities commensurate with their training, often supervising nursing techs and other staff. "There is still a shortage of RNs," says Dacia LeBron, a nurse manager. "We can't train them fast enough. The Bon Secours Memorial College of Nursing helps fill the void. We're expanding into the community with more emphasis on preventative health, such as offering cooking lessons to support healthy eating habits."

As the federal Medicare program shifted from fee-for-service reimbursements to compensation based on quality of patient care, hospitals everywhere struggled to reduce costs without sacrificing quality. One of Ardabell's first initiatives was to survey employees, asking for their ideas on ways to cut costs and improve service in their departments. Managers then voted for the top ten recommendations and implemented them.

Dacia LeBron, who has worked at the hospital for more than a decade, is one of many employees who talk of "the St. Mary's family." "It really is like a family here. We care for each other. There are so many opportunities for a working mom—it's been inspiring for me to see so many women in leadership positions." LeBron is an excellent example of personal growth achieved through St. Mary's educational benefits, earning first an associate degree, then a bachelor's degree, and soon a master's degree as she progressed from patient care technician to LPN to RN. Today she is the nurse manager of a fourteen-bed unit. "It's the mission that we live every day that keeps me here," she says. "You can be open and speak freely about your beliefs. We honor all religions and cultures. I know you don't get that everywhere."

The Evelyn D. Reinhart Guest House opened in 2014 with 16 low-cost guest rooms for the out-of-town families of St. Mary's patients. Volunteers regularly contribute groceries and home-cooked meals for the residents.

A hospital is led by its administration and governing board in partnership with its medical staff to make sure it has the best quality equipment and resources. In early decades, with few exceptions, the physicians affiliated with St. Mary's were not employees of the hospital, but in recent years, a new type of doctor has appeared on the scene, changing the way medical care is delivered. "Hospitalists" are physicians employed by the hospital whose primary focus is the general medical care of hospitalized patients. A patient's care is overseen primarily by a hospitalist rather than his or her own doctor. "When I quit practicing medicine in 1997," says Dr. Larry Zacharias, "there were no hospitalists. Nowadays, a lot of physicians don't even come to the hospital because the ER doctors take care of emergencies and the hospitalists follow the patient during their inpatient stay." Today, St. Mary's employs more than forty hospitalists who cover patient care 24 hours a day, 365 days a year, coordinating with the patient's doctor during the time the patient is in the hospital.

To reinforce its mission of compassionate care, St. Mary's had long offered the use of several small houses located on hospital property to patients' families who lived more than thirty miles outside Richmond. "There were four little white houses on Maple," recalls Nancy Plageman, a former president of volunteers, but as St. Mary's drew patients from an ever-larger geographic area, the demand for overnight housing proved greater than those four houses could handle. "The Reinhart family had donated money in honor of Evelyn Reinhart, [a St. Mary's nurse and volunteer who died of cancer in 1986], to build a large guest house on hospital property for families to stay in while their loved one was in the hospital," says Plageman. "A stipulation provided that the rest of the money would have to be raised within seven years. When Toni Ardabell came to St. Mary's, this became one of her goals, and she came to me and asked if I would chair the fundraising for the remaining two million needed." With co-chair Carmella M. Bladergroen, she took on the project—not an easy sell during a major recession. "We visited other hospitals that had hospitality houses to learn what worked best," she says. Within a short time, they were conferring with architects on the design. The Evelyn D. Reinhart Guest House opened in 2014 with sixteen guest rooms, a double kitchen, a playroom, and several gathering rooms. The modest price of a room is based on the family's ability to pay.

Twenty-first century medicine has gone global. "Richmond is far more international than it ever was," says Dr. Eddy Pizzani, who has been practicing at St. Mary's for more than four decades. "We've adapted to the new demographic. The hospital provides translation now: Chinese, Spanish, Croatian… and we've hired bilingual nurses who speak Spanish." Jean Kerns, retired director of physician services, concurs. "It's practically the United Nations here at St. Mary's. We have doctors from Pakistan, Iran, Africa, Ethiopia, Canada, Australia, Scotland…" In the past few years, PAs (physician assistants) and nurse practitioners have assumed larger roles in the practice of medicine, and midwives have made an appearance at several Bon Secours facilities.

Half a century ago, the federal government instituted two new healthcare programs, Medicare and Medicaid, bringing healthcare to many elderly and poor. Five decades later, the Affordable Care Act went into effect, extending insurance to lower- and middle-income Americans. These two pieces of legislation neatly bookend the story of St. Mary's first fifty years.

The major changes at St. Mary's over its fifty-year lifespan are the same ones that have transformed all American hospitals: astounding leaps in technology and the rise of government regulation. However, Catholic hospitals throughout the country have faced an additional challenge as the number of religious men and women has declined. St. Mary's is not alone in chronicling a steady drop in the number of resident priests and Bon Secours sisters working in the hospital.

"The sisters began handing over responsibilities to laity in a gradual, planned way," recalls Dr. Don Seitz, who began practicing at St. Mary's in 1974 and served as the first lay chairperson of the Bon Secours Health System board from 2010 to 2014. "About ten years ago, a ministry formation program in Marriottsville [Bon Secours headquarters in

Dr. Don Seitz was the first lay chairperson of the Bon Secours Health System board. He served in that capacity from 2010 to 2014.

St. Mary's hired Rhudy & Company to record the recollections of many employees, nuns, and volunteers who worked at the hospital during its first fifty years. These oral histories were archived and edited into a video shown at the fifty-year celebration.

RECONNECTING AFTER FIFTY YEARS

As a member of the book team, Carol Roper Hoffler was afforded the opportunity to reconnect with Sister Rita and relive her own St. Mary's story. A few weeks after the hospital opened, a seriously ill girl was admitted as its 500th patient. Thirteen-year-old Carol had hemorrhaged and was in critical condition with a stomach ailment that baffled the doctors. She remained for a month in a private room on the fourth floor, during which time the sisters gave her the special kind of attention they reserve for children. Carol remembers Sister Rita visiting her room every day, sitting by her bed, holding her hand, and praying for long periods when the situation looked dire. With blood transfusions and care, she gradually recovered her health. "Toward the end of my stay," she recalls, "my sister had an accident and needed surgery, so my parents had two girls in St. Mary's at the same time. When the nurses learned we were sisters, they put an extra bed in my room so we could be together. We had wheelchair races down the halls." Once, Sister Rita took Carol and her mother up to the seventh-floor convent so they could see where she lived and admire the view of Richmond from the picture window. Fifty years later, Carol and Sister Rita met again in Portsmouth, and Carol was able to thank her for all her loving care.

Maryland] began providing an opportunity for lay people to learn about what distinguishes Catholic healthcare from the rest." As the number of sisters in the United States declined, the laity stepped up. "One of the beauties of the reduction in religious members," says Sister Pat Eck, "is that the laity has been called forth. We have recognized and prepared people for leadership. Having said that, we always invite women to join us. We have a number of women in the process in Peru, France, and here in the United States."

The other major change that has taken place in the hospital world is the shift from sick care to healthcare. Hospitals today are beginning to focus as much on healthcare as on sick care, pursuing ways to prevent illness and promote wellness through education and healthy lifestyles. But St. Mary's reached this juncture earlier than most hospitals because its founding mission had always gone beyond the treatment of illness. Ever since 1824, when the first Bon Secours sisters in Paris adopted their holistic approach to patient health, they ventured out of the convent, into the community, and into the home to treat the mind, body, and spirit, and to prevent the spread of illness through education.

Everyone working at St. Mary's today makes a vital contribution to the quality of life of their patients and, through community outreach programs, to people who may never see the inside of the hospital. The coming years will bring an expansion of these community programs, as well as continual improvement in technology and medical practices. "In the future, St. Mary's will become an even stronger beacon of medical excellence, providing not only healthcare, but health, through its programs of illness prevention, health education, and wellness," says Chris Carney.

"St. Mary's has really been the work of God," says Father Duarte, who has visited parishioners in the hospital and celebrated mass there for four decades. "People feel a sense of being cared for by God. Only God could have caused the work of these religious women to be so fruitful. And it's not a work that has been finished. It's really only beginning."

St. Mary's Hospital turns fifty in 2016. Its doctors, nurses, staff, volunteers, and sisters celebrate this landmark with a nod to the past and a vision of the future that inspires generations to come with the Bon Secours mission of compassionate care—"good help for a lifetime."

"I envision only the brightest future for St. Mary's Hospital," said Francine Barr, who has worked at St. Mary's for many years as a nurse, nursing leader, and administrator, and is now chief executive officer. "As we move beyond our 50th year, I see St. Mary's at the forefront of care delivery, focused on meeting the needs of those we serve, whether in our hospital, their homes, or in the community. The caliber of our physician and nursing teams, the level of care we provide, and our ability to care for generations of people will only improve."

Sister Pat Eck has lived and worked at St. Mary's, on and off, since 1968. The changes she has witnessed have been profound, and she sees no end to them. "What happens in the future depends on the needs of the community," she says. "St. Mary's lives up to its name of Good Help. It responds to God's call. Many organizations do that, of course, but St. Mary's has a long history of caring for people. People leave there knowing they are loved… God calls us to be one with God by recognizing our own gifts and responding to that call. For me, the charism [spiritual orientation] of Bon Secours is compassion, healing, and liberation. Compassion leads to healing leads to liberation," she explains. "From the beginning of life to the end of life, it's who we are, and we do it very well at St. Mary's."

"I've always felt close to the nuns at St. Mary's. I celebrated my second mass after my ordination in the small nun's chapel on the seventh floor. And the nuns took care of my father—Sister Pat and Sister Rose Marie came down in the middle of the night to be on either side of me when he died."

—Father Scott Duarte

Francine Barr, formerly chief nursing officer and chief operating officer of St. Mary's, was named CEO in 2015, making her the ninth administrator in the hospital's history.

ST. MARY'S HOSPITAL ADMINISTRATORS

Mother Germanus, 1961–1967

Sister Rita Thomas, 1967–1972

Richard D. O'Hallaron, 1972–1987

Christopher M. Carney, 1987–1992

Sharon Tanner, 1992–1996

Ann E. Honeycutt, 1996–2001

Michael Kerner, 2001–2008

Toni Ardabell, 2009–2015

Francine Barr, 2015–present

BON SECOURS RICHMOND HEALTH SYSTEM CEOS

Christopher Carney 1992–1997
  (1997–2005 CEO Bon Secours U.S.)

John Simpson 1997–2000

Peter Bernard 2000–2015

Toni Ardabell 2015–present

PRESIDENTS OF THE MEDICAL STAFF: 1966–2015

1966–1967	Dr. Edwin L. Kendig, Jr.
1968–1969	Dr. Joseph F. Kell, Jr.
1970–1971	Dr. Charles Riley
1972–1976	Dr. Charles M. Zacharias
1977–1979	Dr. Ernest B. Carpenter
1980–1983	Dr. Austin B. Harrelson,
1984–1987	Dr. Lawrence C. Zacharias
1988–1989	Dr. Read McGehee, Jr.
1990–1991	Dr. Yale H. Zimberg
1992–1993	Dr. George A. Knaysi
1994–1995	Dr. Donald G. Seitz
1996–1997	Dr. Thomas D. Davis, Jr.
1998–1999	Dr. Charles H. Robertson
2000–2001	Dr. Robert J. Cohen
2002–2003	Dr. Kenneth Olshansky
2004–2005	Dr. Gan Dunnington
2006–2007	Dr. Michael Mandel
2008–2009	Dr. Gregg L. Londrey
2010–2011	Dr. George A. Parker
2012–2013	Dr. Julious Smith, III
2014–2015	Dr. Richard Szucs

SISTERS WHO SERVED AT ST. MARY'S HOSPITAL, RICHMOND, VA

Sr. Germanus Streett [1961–1967; *founder of Richmond community, oversaw construction and opening of St. Mary's Hospital, 1st hospital administrator*]

Sr. Mary Margaret Burger [1961–1964; *Richmond community pioneer, public health nursing*]

Sister Mary of the Incarnation Muntean [1961; *Richmond community pioneer, home nursing*]

Sr. Clare of Assisi McGee [1962–1966; *nursing*]

Sister Francis Helen Lewandowski [1964–1966, 1976–1977, 1980, 1982–2005; *auxiliary, administrator, sister visitor, hospital volunteer*]

Sister Rita Thomas (Xavier) [1964–1973; *director of nursing services, administrator*]

Sister Rose O'Brien [1965–2005; *instructor-School of Medical Technology, chief medical technologist, board member, medical technician*]

Sister Mary Monica Curley [1965–1995; *medical record administrator, board of directors, auxiliary, librarian, receptionist, sister visitor*]

Sister Bernadette Maureen Rogers (Sister Mary Catherine) [1965–1973; *nursing supervisor-OB, med-surg nurse, CCU*]

Sister Mary Emma Carroll [1965–1971; *nursing*]

Sister Mary Gemma Neville [1965–1969; *supervisor-surgery*]

Sister Margaret Louise Nugent [1966–1969; *nursing instructor*]

Sister Elizabeth Durney [1966–1976, 1978–1994; *assistant director of nursing, med-surg supervisor, pastoral care associate, thanatologist, board of directors, founder & director of Bon Secours Chez Vous, patient advocate, community health liaison, mission board*]

Sister James Marie Higgins [1967; *nursing*]

Sister Patricia Eck [1968–1975, 1979, 1985–1997; *operating-room nurse, surgical coordinator; chief operating officer, senior VP, VP-mission & quality, president St. Mary's & BSHSI boards*]

Sister Mary James Keating [1968–1971; *X-ray technician*]

Sister Justine Cyr [1968–1969; *nursing & administration*]

Sister Thomas Magdalen Carney (Eileen) [1968; *nursing*]

Sister Roselle Lintner [1969; *lab technician*]

Sister Martha Jenkins [1969–1971; *EKG-business office*]

Sister Rose Marie Jasinski [1970–1983; *nursing, head nurse-surgery, staff nurse-IVNA & home health program*]

Sister Mary Imelda Titus [1970–1971; *sister visitor*]

Sister Mary Theresa Mullin [1973; *head nurse*]

Sister Mary Ruth Fox [1973; *administration*]

Sister Frances McCabe [1973; *administrative offices intern*]

Sister Elaine Davia [1973–1984; *nursing, mobile health unit staff & director*]

Sister Rosemarie Iserman [1973–1977; *administration, board president*]

Sister Angela Neville [1975–1978, 1981; *nursing*]

Sister Mary Shimo [1977–1983; *chaplain, pastoral care department*]

Sister Mary Ellen Pietrowski [1977–1980; *pediatric nursing assistant*]

Sister Patricia Dowling [1977–1979; *unit manager, administrative intern*]

Sister Sharon Paige [1977–1979; *nursing*]

Sister Dianne Decubellis [1977–1979; *medication technician*]

Sister Patricia Clossey [1977–1978; *psych-OT*]

Sister Mary McLaughlin [1978; *candidacy program*]

Sister Victoria Segura [1979–1980, 2000–present; *pathologist, medical director of hospice and palliative medicine, president of Joint Hospitals board of directors.*]

Sister Dorothy Brogan [1981–1989; *pastoral associate, board of directors, home pastoral program*]

Sister Dorothy Marie Cary [1981; *hospice study*]

Sister Nancy Glynn [1987–1990; *director-mission effectiveness*]

Sister Jean Aulenback [1988–1992; *hospice & home health*]

Sister Anne Marie Mack [2004–present; *VP-mission*]

Sister Mary Brigid Tembo [2005; *novitiate program*]

✦ ACKNOWLEDGMENTS ✦

This book could not have been written without the dozens of people who shared their memories and explained "how things worked back then." Special thanks go to Anne S. Napps, project coordinator, who organized the entire research effort, scheduled interviews, dug up obscure facts, reviewed early drafts, and gave solid advice—all the while maintaining an unfailingly cheerful attitude.

Toni Ardabell
Sister Jean Aulenback
Francine Barr
Beverly Beck
Lloyd Bell
Peter Bernard
Kathy Bond
Julie Bondy
Joseph Borzelleca
Debra Broderick
Megan Buchan
Gennette Cameron-Reid
Christopher Carney
Idamae Claiborne
Sister Elaine Davia
Tommy Davis, MD
Mary Ruth DeForest
Christine DeLaughter
Earlean Didlake
Sister Patricia Dowling
Father J. Scott Duarte
Susanne Duff
Anne Dunnington
Sister Patricia Eck
Stanley Goldman, MD
Jennifer Goins

Jean Grogan
Mary Halsted
Ron and Tonya Harris
Mary Herbert
Ann E. Honeycutt
Sister Rose Marie Jasinski
Melissa Jones
Gerald Katz
Michael Kerner
Jean Kerns
George Knaysi, MD
Nellie League
Dacia LeBron
Steve Lindsey
Sister Anne Marie Mack
Marian Mahon
Kathryn O. Mauch
Pete McCourt
Read McGehee, MD
Shari Morris
Mary Ann Mugal
John J. Muldowney
Roger Neathawk
Gene Oakey
Richard O'Hallaron
George Parker, MD

Eddy Pizzani, MD
Miriam Pizzani, MD
Nancy Plageman
Bill Portes
Ella Randolph
Don Seitz, MD
Sister Vicki Segura
Mary Ann Sheehan
Donna Shifflett
Rev. Msgr. Thomas F. Shreve
Brent and Allison Spiller
Andrea Springer
Richard Statuto
Sofia Teferi, MD
Sister Rita Thomas
Kathy Thompson
Mary Washbourne
Ralph Wheeler
Barbara Thalhimer
William B. Thalhimer III
Bill Upton
L. Douglas Wilder
Tiffany Wilson
Larry Zacharias, MD
Barbara Zohab
Patrick Anthony Zohab